GIACOMO BALLA

AN ALBUM
OF HIS LIFE AND WORK

GIACOMO BALLA

BY VIRGINIA DORTCH DORAZIO

AN ALBUM OF HIS LIFE AND WORK

INTRODUCTION BY
GIUSEPPE UNGARETTI

ALFIERI

SBN 8150-0405-2
Library of Congress Catalog Card Number 70140146

Printed in Italy by Fantonigrafica ® Venice

For K.M.D. + R.L.D.

One afternoon in the early autumn of 1952, I went with an Italian friend to visit Giacomo Balla at home in his studio in Rome. In the midst of the multi-colored objects which crowded the sun-lit salon, the octogenarian Balla sat in a checkered armchair with a plaid blanket over his knees. No longer able to work standing up, he sat there sketching, his gray head slightly inclined, his blue eyes penetrating and optimistic. With the hand of an old master, he was making free-line drawings of landscapes from memory. Behind him was a Futurist cabinet and chair which he had designed himself and painted in bright green and yellow patterns.

A confused background of intense colors and a variety of curious shapes and forms surrounded him. Focusing my attention on each object in turn, I slowly perceived an enormous diversity of paintings and sculpture mixed in together with regular household objects. Large and small paintings in the Divisionist technique hung together on one wall. I recognized the artist's self-portrait in a heavy wooden frame resting on an easel. Painted by Balla in his mature years, it showed him drinking a cup of Italian coffee. In a corner near the door was another, smaller portrait which he had painted in his youth. It portrayed only his nude right shoulder.

Silhouetted against the translucent curtain of a window was a wooden smoker's table with its irregular levels, designed by Balla to be light-weight and easily movable. Turning to look down the brilliant red, yellow, green, violet, and blue hallway, I could see the telephone sitting in an alcove with a small table and stool, both brightly painted in abstract shapes. A blue wood 'mobile' from Balla's Futurist days was suspended from the top of an open doorway. Here and there were Futurist flower sculptures; on a desk was a Futurist letter holder. The brightly colored ceramic tile floor was composed of abstract shapes designed by Balla, while the Futurist rug was handwoven after a design by Balla. His own Futurist waistcoat hung by a hangar on the wall.

Luce and Elica, his two daughters, brought out all kinds of objects wrapped in tissue paper for us to see. There were dozens and dozens of carefully preserved drawings among which were projects for sculpture, for pieces of furniture, for interiors. Various Futurist objects included 'modificanti' or dress modifiers, and a Futurist tie. There were a small series of abstract watercolors and several pocket-size notebooks.

Then tea was served on a Futurist tray painted by Balla in his familiar bright green and yellow. The conversation which took place over tea was in Italian, and as I had been in Italy only a short time at that point, I could understand very little of what was said. While I wished in some ways this had not been so, still in another sense I was glad that I was not obliged to interrupt the almost totally visual experience of this first visit by participating in polite conversation. Consequently, I was more or less at liberty to let my eyes study Balla and his world about which I was later to learn much more.

While Balla's work was at that time limited mainly to drawings because of poor health, all his hand-made tools lay close by. In one corner of the room was a working lamp which he had used to illuminate the lower portions of his canvases. Hunks of hand-made brushes were stuffed upside-down in tin cans which were also painted in strong colors and abstract shapes. There were all kinds of tools: some for making frames or table easels, and even a hand-made hammer.

Luce showed us a series of important Futurist paintings which were still in the studio, unbought und unnoticed by contemporary critics. Some had been lying sideways, and piled up in rows three or four deep. Among them were some of his early abstract studies of light which he called 'iridescent interpenetrations'. By this time, I could well understand why Balla was known as the 'Color Magician'.

In those days, Balla still had the original sculpture entitled 'Boccioni's Fist — Lines of Force' in his studio. It was a cardboard construction painted bright red, and it was standing on a table near the sofa in the salon. At first glance it looked to me like a purely abstract construction, but I was told that Balla meant it to represent a human configuration in motion, and then I could see the force of Boccioni's arms and legs as he moved through space.

Everywhere my eye fell in his studio, there were signs of his dream of a 'Futurist Universe' becoming a reality — although on a very limited scale. The fact that almost all the household objects were of an original Futurist design revealed Balla's desire to provide 'art for everyone'.

During this first visit, I took several photographs, but I think that the effect of all those vivid shapes and colors in the presence of that gentle man made an even greater impression on my memory. Some years later, shortly after Balla's death in 1958, I began to collect information and photographs with the idea of making an album visually relating Balla's paintings with his Roman environment and experiences.

I began questioning Balla's friends and, above all, his daughters, Luce and Elica. I wanted to know the 'where, when, and why' of every one of Balla's creations that I had seen. I felt the answers were not only interesting, but important for an understanding of Balla's art, and so I have presented them in the album in a sequence of photographs chronologically relating the story of the artist's life and work.

Balla is justly famous for his research in the area of light and motion. His almost scientific interest in the relationships of certain natural phenomena led him to observe, analyze and afterwards paint the various optical effects of light and color, of light on color, and of the color of light. His studies of human beings, animals and machines in motion were original aesthetic expressions of the Futurists' initial concepts which Balla was to develop from reality to abstract symbols, so that for speed, vortexes, noises, and even smells he conceived essential and unique symbols.

Yet, what I have found most fascinating is that Balla was concerned with the emotion, as well as the motion of the human body. His paintings of moods or 'stati d'animo' reveal an intuitive exploration of the subconscious. His desire to give formal expression to such intangibles recalls his favorite phrase, *L'Impalpabile Andamentale* or 'Impalpable Continuous Motion' — that something which you cannot touch, which is no longer there. It can be the path of movement of a person or a bird or a car. It can even be the movement of an observer watching another moving object. Balla recognized the existence of the *L'Impalpabile Andamentale* and he painted it.

It is my hope that this album of Balla's life and work, while lacking Balla's magic color, should be primarily a stimulating visual experience for the reader, compelling him to a more rewarding investigation of Balla.

This book would not have been possible without the patience and generosity of Luce and Elica Balla. I am particularly indebted to Giuseppe Ungaretti for providing the introduction.

Virginia Dortch Dorazio

Rome, 1969

Balla, nome indimenticabile, nome festoso, verso la festosità quasi come per insorgenza di forzatura molesta, certo indiscreta, sorprendente a designare un uomo che fu sempre d'una discrezione persino eccessiva, bonario uomo, persino troppo, nei personali e familiari rapporti: in ogni rapporto suo col prossimo, anche se fu uno dei rari chiamato ad accorgersi che anche nelle arti tutto era in via di mutarsi da capo a fondo.

Nome indimenticabile, eppure da tanto tempo, se da pochi ancora, intensamente e fruttuosamente rammentato, consultandolo, e preso a modello, per la poesia del suo segno, per la precisione implacabile del suo segno poetico, dai più non dico ridotto all'oblio, ma quasi ignorato se non per quel momento, che si considera ancora dai più di scandalo o di beffa, quando qualche opera sua appariva nella mostra dei Futuristi e il suo nome nei loro manifesti.

Eppure il pittore Balla è oggi considerato, dai pochi che s'intendono d'arte, e specialmente di pittura, e sono sempre stati pochi, e le dita di una mano sono state sempre troppe per indicarne l'esiguo numero — eppure il pittore Giacomo Balla si considera da quella scarsissima schiera di veri intenditori, il pittore italiano più dotato e di maggiore forza espressiva dei suoi tempi: uno dunque dei maggiori pittori, dei quattro o cinque maggiori del nostro secolo pittorico europeo.

Chi ne ha esaminato la sua prima posizione in arte, discorre di influssi di Previati o di Segantini, e poi, più tardi, giunge fino a citare Klimt: parla di Balla come di uno che si era avvicinato presto al Divisionismo, e Gino Severini ricorda, nella propria autobiografia, che Balla si era, e in modo precoce, accostato difatti al Divisionismo.

C'è però da osservare, ed è forse per questo che quasi subito lo seduce il prestigio della comparsa in pittura delle ricerche del Divisionismo: il valore preminente da conferire in ogni caso alla luce. Anche nelle sue opere di principiante, la prima mira che conquisti un netto orientamento nella sua ricerca è l'intervento fondamentale da lui conferito all'effetto di luce: semplicemente un'impronta di luce qua e là, a volte quasi un divorare della luce, dove occorre che la luce intervenga risolutiva: e difatti la luce incomincia a risolvere presto i suoi problemi espressivi.

Luce. Sotto il segno della luce è sorto Balla, questo nostro grande pittore, quando avverrà che la luce incominci a travolgerne sempre più l'ispirazione, inducendolo a raggiungere l'originalità e la grandezza: è fatto che non tarderà per lui molto ad avvenire.

Luce, e potenza, e con quale potenza, appena in quel suo nascere alla pittura, affronta subito la realtà, e sarà, in quel suo iniziale entrare in giuoco, una potenza espressiva di solidarietà umana, anche se manifestata nei modi dei suoi tempi dell'arte, dettati più dal cuore che da una presenza d'un'evoluzione inflessibile della edificazione scientificamente umana della società — ammesso che la scienza possa contenere in sè tutto e non la travalicherà sempre un mistero.

Nel 1905, quando il nostro pittore era ancora agli esordi, dipinge difatti quel pastello su carta, quel dittico, come dirà, « I piedi della Signora e della Pazza », e si guardi quale significato assumono quei piedi, quelli di profilo elegante che si svolge dagli stivaletti chic, confrontati a quegli altri, della misera, nelle ciabatte troppo vaste, sotto rozze, eppure azzurre, calze cascanti.

La realtà dovrà apparirgli presto in un modo più inflessibile, nel processo, nel progresso, nel suo tremendo, e a volte può apparire orrendo, evolversi e trasformarsi per opera dei progredienti mezzi che vanno vertiginosamente gli uomini foggiandosi per le neces-

sità crescenti di una società in mutamento dalle fondamenta, almeno da quelle materiali — certo non mai dal fondamento spirituale dell'uomo, non potendo mai, essendo fondamentale, ridursi a farsi di natura materiale, anche se ad essa natura materiale è connesso, in essa coinvolto, per tutta la durata dell'esistenza, intimamente da essa stretto e costretto, per emanciparsene di continuo, almeno. Aderisce al Futurismo, si allea ai Futuristi nel 1909. Boccioni e Severini gli erano stati discepoli a Roma, e gli volevano molto bene ancora e gliene vorranno sempre, e lo consideravano anche dopo la sua adesione al Futurismo, più che compagno, sempre il maestro. Ma con Boccioni ci sarà subito una presa di becco, nell'interpretazione futurista dell'arte, almeno in relazione a quella del primo modo d'intenderla da parte di Balla. Per il primo Balla futurista, il movimento, nel suo dinamismo, può riflettersi in pittura nella rappresentazione oggettiva di un oggetto, figura di persona o di cosa, insistendo sulla diversità, mentre esso oggetto si va muovendo, raggiunta nonostante la fretta del suo mutarsi: Balla raggiunge così il voluto effetto sovrapponendo uno dopo l'altro il susseguirsi dei movimenti d'un medesimo oggetto osservato negli intervalli ridotti a estrema brevità, del suo muoversi. Boccioni protestava, accusando quella un'analisi vana, da fotografo cineasta, mentre per lui, Boccioni, per lui Boccioni il Futurismo, si trattava di rappresentare la realtà nella sintesi del suo moto, come un momento unico, non come una serie di successivi momenti, come un momento di realtà tanto nuova e originale da essere unicamente riinvenzione totale della realtà, ogni volta oggetto assolutamente nuovo, e da tutto alla fine emancipato e indipendente, di tutto insomma sintesi assoluta.

Non fu una polemica di lunga durata, e Balla aveva altri motivi, anche nel periodo strettamente futurista: l'ispirazione gli sarebbe continuata a venire dalla luce, in modo che andava ormai provando sempre meglio attraverso ogni filtro, per possedere sempre meglio un occhio netto, imparando a godere sempre meglio dei miracoli della luce.

Dove Balla sia arrivato, è agevole oggi dirlo, da chi sa, da quelli, e sono ancora pochi, si è già detto, che sanno come in pittura stiano veramente le cose. Arriva più in là, di certo, infinitamente più in là dei Divisionisti, ma arriva più in là persino dagli Impressionisti, non direi di Seurat, autentico principe della pittura; ma Seurat è di legame impressionista, è tutt'altra personalità, non vanno fatti, per carità, sterili confronti. E vorrei anche s'intendessero bene che, parlando di Balla, non intendo varcare i suoi tempi, e lo meriterebbe, essendo, di quelli successivi, nostri, per numerose vie, uno dei precursori. E non lo inserirò dunque quelli nostri — quelli nostri che vanno dall'ultima guerra in poi, e da un po' prima, e che valgono specie per le loro particolari traversie.

Già, certo, l'inseguimento di sè stessa da parte d'una figura di persona, poteva suggerire al pittore d'indurne gli aspetti a compenetrarsi, dando di essi, nella loro minima varietà, la cinematica: qui il tocco pittorico, i tocchettini pittorici di Balla, sono all'altezza già d'un Seurat. Ma Balla non si è fermato qui. Si osservi che novità venga subito a rappresentare, Balla, dopo l'adesione al Futurismo del 1910, com'è subito più furente, più occulto, più vero, e — giacchè prediligevano tale parola i suoi alleati della nuova scuola — più dinamismo di ogni altro Futurista, e forse di qualsiasi altro pittore sino ad oggi. Si guardi l'abbaglio, fremente, impaziente, fulmineo e fulminante, della « Lampada ad arco »: è del 1909. Si guardino le « Mani della violinista »: sono del 1912: si guardi la sublime delicatezza del tratteggio che ne fa risaltare la corsa sulle corde, sottile tratteggio, oserei dire tatuaggio, magico, medianico. Fino dal 1912, anche se l'ossessione del susseguirsi compenetrantesi d'un medesimo oggetto persiste, per esempio, nelle « Mani della violinista », già si colloca in alto, in prima fila, sul palco dei maggiori inventori dell'arte di questo secolo.

E il « Dinamismo d'un cane al guinzaglio »? E' ancora un dipinto del 1912. Quel cagnolo che diventa, camminando, di pelo elettrico, che non è più che elettrizzato e elettrizzante moto, nonostante il guinzaglio, anch'esso fattosi catena, rete isterica di moto. Il moto, certo il moto, ma il moto che si risolve in luce, l'apparizione della luce, la sorpresa, il miracolo nel moto dell'apparizione rivelatrice della luce.

Dal 1912 al 1916, è la fase del Nostro che chiameremo « futurista », la sua fase che alla buona può chiamarsi la fase che ha per oggetto il dinamismo, il dinamismo per scomposizioni della luce che rivelano gli oggetti, per colori, per impulsività e impulso d'ogni minima striscia di colore volta nella sua spinta all'unità, a ricomporre la luce da essa franta, mirando nella sua complessità, nel suo unico definitivo risultato e effetto a luce: scomposizioni della luce in tutte le loro possibilità a probabilità di colore, disintegrazione della luce in colori offerti dagli oggetti osservati, per indurla a potersi riedificare nel medesimo attimo quale integrità di luce, non più nell'abbaglio, via via che il pittore progredisce nei suoi risultati, ma in luce che è rivelazione oggettiva di sè stessa, ricomponendosi subitaneamente, fusione improvvisa di quei colori nei quali, per necessità di espressione pittorica, era andata prima scindendosi.

Seguendo tale orientamento l'opera di Balla va dal 1912 al 1916.

Potremmo soffermarci a quelle opere, a quegli incendi del colore che simili a furenti insofferenze e impazienze, serpeggiano come sotto la cenere, e finiscono col conquistare in sè, nei loro lampeggiamenti, nei loro taurini scontri, nel loro ferirsi a vicenda, nei loro schianti e nella loro ira, impietosa senza smetterla mai — e finiscono coll'imporre a quelle opere, a ciascuna di esse via via con maggiori precauzioni e più stupefacenti risultati, di ritrovarsi, di ricongiungersi nel segreto impulso e volere, di riconoscersi insomma unicamente alla fine, come raggiunta, conquistata, domata, macerante, beatificante assolutezza di luce.

Le corposità invadono gli spazi, sono durezza, sono flessibilità, sono lievissimo alito. Vi vanno succedendo, vi si assottigliano, sono nastri, sono costrette a farsi volte, lastre di metallo durissimo, sono accartocciamenti, sono spirali che si consumano, che si compiono ascendendo perfette, nella brutalità del loro immenso garbo. Insomma tutto, in tanta varietà, e scontri, e avventurarsi, e avventarsi, e violarsi, e contorcersi, e farsi d'acciaio, e farsi di latta, e farsi di piuma, e farsi di nulla, tutto, insomma, senza mai smettere di proseguire la sua irosa voluttà di muoversi, di agitarsi, di slargarsi, di assottigliarsi, di subire, quanto più ci si rifiuti la materia, la costrizione a riduzione in volta, di definirsi insomma: tutta questa materia d'una realtà attuale, oggettiva e profetica, tremendamente profetica, tutta questa materia risolta sulle tele in colori, in zuffa di colori, non ha che una mira, una sola, divenire in ultima analisi luce, somma che non sprigioni se non luce: diviene difatti, per chi sappia contemplare quelle opere, estrema, ultima, sublime realtà di luce.

Dovrei aggiungere altro. Mi ci vorrebbe, e anche sino a qui mi ci sarebbe voluta, l'eloquenza che meritano quelle opere, l'originalità inventiva dell'opera di Balla, la sua presenza incomparabile nella storia della pittura.

Dal 1916, l'arte di Balla si apre un altro varco, entra in un altro cielo. Non sono più gli oggetti ad ispirarlo, cerca l'ispirazione in sè, negli stati del suo animo. S'interiorizza, si propone di abolire la realtà esterna. Gli sarà possibile. Lo sforzo è sovrumano, gli effetti uguagliano i precedenti, li sorpassano e dicono una parola nuova, già anch'essi, nonostante qualsiasi proposito di suprema, tirate le somme, eloquenza interiore.

Forse dunque nulla è mutato, salvo il riferimento, di proposito negato, agli oggetti circostanti, salvo il riferimento che più non pretende di essere che di ordine e di carattere psicologici. C'è tuttavia ora un'intensificazione nei risultati. C'è una maggiore complicatezza nel riassumere le forme dei vari colori chiamati a interpretare la volontà dell'artista, e a fondersi alla fine in luce per chiarirne interiormente l'animo.

Insomma, anche ora, nel periodo che si chiude nel 1924, il risultato, eccelso, che compendia, che riassume, che assomma, che definisce, in modo all'estremo franto, quasi troppo frazionato, tutti gli sforzi e i risultati della nuova ricerca, inoltrata dentro di sè, strappata unicamente da dentro di sè, abolita ogni osservazione oggettiva, ogni ispirazione e ogni stimolo che gli accorrevano incontro una volta dalla realtà oggettiva — anch'essa, estrema esperienza, non ha altre pretese per lui che fare luce in lui, e, alla fine, diviene anch'essa unicamente luce, come tutta la sua pittura. Luce! Luce! Luce!

Balla, Giacomo Balla, grande, grande, grande pittore: vero pittore. Non di frequente si è veri pittori, anche in quei secoli nei quali vissero quelli da tutti chiamati, indistintamente, sovente balordamente, grandi, e che non sono spessissimo che molto minuscoli pittori, se non addirittura i deformi della pittura.

Roma, dal 10 al 20 maggio 1968

Giuseppe Ungaretti

Balla, an unforgettable name, a festive name that leaps with an energy almost molesting, certainly indiscrete, an astonishing name for a man who was always discrete, excessively so, a man kindly to a fault within his family and with his friends, in every relation, in short, with his fellow man, even though he was one of those rare beings who have the gift to perceive that even in the arts everything is in a state of fundamental change.

An unforgettable name, but for some time now, if he has been intensely and fruitfully remembered by a few, who have studied him and who have used him as their model because of the poetry of his line, the implacable precision of his poetic mark, yet by the many I do not say he has been reduced to oblivion but certainly he has been ignored except on those rare occasions when he is re-examined as a figure of scandal or of derision whenever a work of his appeared in an exhibition of the Futurists or his name in their manifestoes.

And yet the painter Balla is today considered by the few who know anything about art, and especially about painting — and they have always been few, the finger of one hand being more than enough to point out their scant number — yet the painter Giacomo Balla, I say, is considered by that rare band of true connoisseurs to be the Italian painter most in tune with his times and expressed their spirit most forcefully. He was, therefore, one of the great painters, one of the four or five major painters of our European pictorial century.

Those who have studied his leading position in art speak of the movements of Previati or of Segantini and then later they come to Klimt and they speak of Balla as one who approached Divisionism. Gino Severini recalls in his autobiography that Balla was in fact precociously close to Divisionism.

One must, however, keep in mind — and this is perhaps the reason that he was almost immediately seduced by the glamourous appearance in painting of the aims of Divisionism — the pre-eminent value he always placed on light. Even in his earliest paintings the first objective that may convince one of a clear-cut direction in his development is his fundamental introduction of the effect of light, simply a trace of light here and there, at times almost a gobbling up of light, where it happens that the light comes through resolutely and where in fact he soon begins to solve his problems of expression.

Light. Balla, this great painter of ours, rose under the sign of light when he realized that light began to sweep on his inspiration ever more strongly, leading him to achieve originality and greatness, and it is a fact that he was not slow in achieving these.

Light and power and with that power even in his first emergence as a painter, he at once confronted reality, and it was, in his first entering into the lists, a power expressive of human solidarity, even if it manifested itself in the artistic styles of his day, which were dictated more by the heart than by the presence of an inflexible evolution of the scientific insight of man into society, admitting that science may contain all within itself and will leave no mystery unsolved.

In 1905 when our painter was still in his beginnings he painted, in fact, that pastel on paper, that diptych, as it is called, « I piedi della Signora e della Pazza », and one can see what significance those feet assume, those of an elegant profile in chic boots confronting those others of the poor infortunate in their oversized, worn-out shoes under rough, blue bagging stockings.

Reality must have appeared to him early in a more inflexible way in his procession, in his progression, in his tremendous, and at times his seemingly horrendous evolution and transformation through works of improving techniques, in which people move dizzily, shaped by their necessities, reared in a society that was changing in its fundamentals, at least in its material aspect, certainly not in its spiritual aspect, which can never, being fundamental, reduce itself to become material, even if the material is linked with it, entwined with it throughout the eternity of existence, clasped to it and impelled continuously to free itself.

He turned to Futurism and allied himself to the Futurists in 1909. Boccioni and Severini had been his disciples in Rome and they loved him and will always love him and consider him even after his adherence to Futurism more than a comrade, always the master. But with Boccioni there was an immediate bickering over the futuristic interpretation of art, at least with respect to Balla's first understanding of it. For the first Futuristic Balla movement, in its dynamism, could be reflected in painting in the objective representation of an object, the form of a person or thing, by emphasizing its diversity of elements, as this object was in the process of movement, notwithstanding the speed of its changing. Balla thus achieved his desired effect by placing in sequence one after the other the movements of the same object observed at the intervals of its movement, these being reduced to extreme briefness. Boccioni protested, attacking the analysis as vain and cinematographic, whereas for him, Boccioni, for Boccioni the Futuristissimo it was a question of representing reality in the synthesis of its motion as a unique moment, not as a series of successive movements, but as a moment of reality so new and original as to be uniquely a total reinvention of reality, each time the object totally new and in the end emancipated from everything else and independent, an absolute synthesis, in short of all.

It was not a polemic of long duration, and Balla had other objectives even in this his strictly futuristic period: the inspiration that continued to come to him from light that led him to go seeking ever more keenly through every filter to possess an ever clearer eye and to learn to enjoy ever more deeply the miracles of light.

Just where Balla may have arrived is easy to say for him who knows, for those, and they are still few, as has already been pointed out, who know how things really stand in painting. He went further, certainly, infinitely further than the Divisionists, but he went even beyond the Impressionists, though not, I should say, beyond Seurat, the authentic prince of painting. But Seurat is of the true impressionist line, quite another personality, not to make, for heaven's sake, sterile comparisons. And I should like it well understood that speaking of Balla, I do not intend to overstep his era, though he would deserve it, being one of the precursors in so many ways of those who followed him, those of our day. And so I shall not include him with our painters — those of ours who have risen after the last war and even a little bit before, and who are especially worthwhile for their particular mishaps.

Certainly, the very pursuit of oneself on the part of a human figure could suggest to a painter to bring its aspects to interpenetrate when dealing with their minimal variation, the cinematographic. Here the pictorial touch, the tiny little touches of Balla are of the order of a Seurat. But Balla did not stop there. Observe what novelty Balla began to depict immediately after his adherence to Futurism in 1910, how he immediately was more furious, more occult, more truthful and — since his comrades in the new school had a predilection for such words — more dynamic than any other Futurist and even perhaps of any other painter up to the present time. Note the brilliance, throbbing, impatient, flashing and lightening-like, of the « Lampada ad arco », done in 1909. Observe the « Mani del violinista » of 1912. Note the sublime delicate line that shows the run across the chords, a subtle drawing that I even dare call tattooing, magical, mediumistic. Already by 1912 even if the obsession to achieve the interpenetration of the same object persisted, as for example in the « Mani del violinista », still he must take his place up high in a box in the first tier with the major originators in art of this century.

And the « Dinamismo d'un cane al guinzaglio »? It is still a painting of 1912. That little dog's fur, while it is walking, bristles, it is really electrified and electrifying motion in spite of the leash, which itself has become a chain, a hysterical net of motion. Motion, certainly motion, but motion which resolves itself in light! The apparition of light! From 1912 to 1916 was the phase of Balla's life that we shall call « futuristic », his phase which at its best can be called the phase that had dynamism as its object, the dynamism for the breaking up of light to reveal objects, for colors, spontaneity and the impulse of every least trace of color that thrusts toward unity, all to recompose the light broken up by these, aiming in its complexity, in its simple definite result and effect at light: the decompositions of light in all their possibilities and probabilities of colors, the disintegration of light into the colors presented by observed objects, to induce it to reconstruct the same instant that wholeness of light, no longer in the brilliance, the more the painter progresses in his results, but in a light that is an objective revelation of itself, recomposing itself instantly, a sudden fusion of those colors into which, because of the requirements of pictorial expression, it had first divided itself.

The work of Balla followed this trend from 1912 to 1916. We could linger over these works, over those flames of color that like intolerant and impatient furies that seem to twist and turn under the ashes and end up by conquering in themselves, in their lightening-bolts, in their taurine encounters, in their wounding of each other, in their crashing and in their ire, unpitying and unending, and they end up by forcing these works, each one of them with ever greater care and more stunning results, to find themselves, to meet themselves anew in a secret impluse and will, to recognize themselves, in short, uniquely in the end as a captured, conquered, tamed, macerating and beatifying absoluteness of light.

The bodies invade the spaces, they are hardness, flexibility, the lightest breath. They come one after the other, drawing out to a thinness, they are ribbons, they are forced to bend themselves in curves, slabs of hardest metal, they are like wrapping paper, spirals that consume themselves, that end up rising to perfection in the coarseness of their immense form. In short, all in endless variety, the crashes, the venturing, the hurling, the being violated, the contorting, the becoming steel and the becoming tin, and feather, and nothing, all in short, without ever interrupting their furious delight in moving, acting, broadening, thinning out, obeying the more their material form is denied, the compulsion to reduce their flight, in defining themselves, in short. All this matter of an actual reality, objective and prophetic, tremendously prophetic, all this matter results on the canvas in colors, in a brawl of colors, and this has only one aim, one alone, to become in the last analysis light. It becomes, in fact, for him who knows how to look at these works, the extreme, ultimate, sublime reality of light.

Is there anything else to add? If only I had, just as up to now I ought to have had, the eloquence merited by these works, the inventive originality of Balla's work and his incomparable presence in the history of painting.

From 1916 Balla's art took a new turn. It entered another realm. Objects no longer inspired him. He sought inspiration within himself, in the realms of his mind. He turned inwards and proposed to abolish external reality. Was this possible? The effort was superhuman, and yet the effects at least equaled the preceding ones. They even surpassed them and spoke a new message, whatever purpose supreme interior eloquence may have had.

Perhaps nothing is changed, except the reference, willfully denied, to the surrounding objects, except the reference that pretends to be only to order and to psychological characters. There is now above all an intensification of the results. There is a greater complication in reassuming the forms of the various colors called upon to interpret the will of the artist and to melt in the end into light to clarify internally the spirit.

In short, even here in the period that ends in 1924 the sublime result, that epitomizes, that sums up, that defines in a manner of extreme fracturing, almost too fractured, all the forces and results of his new quest deep inside himself, uniquely pulled out from within himself, with every objective observation abolished, every inspiration and every stimulus that brought him into contact at one time with objective reality — even this quest, this extreme experience has no other meaning for him but to make light within himself and in the end to become itself uniquely light, like all his painting. Light! Light! Light!

Balla, Giacomo Balla, great, great, great painter — true painter. Not often are there true painters even in those centuries when there lived those who are called by all, confusedly, often mistakenly, great and who are most often only very minor painters, if not actually destroyers of painting.

Rome, May 1 oth 2oth, 1968   Giuseppe Ungaretti

1

1. *Line of Speed* (Synthesis) (1913). Ink on paper,
11 3/4 x 17 3/4 inches. Collection Zack, Toronto.
Balla considered this drawing fundamental to
his Futurist concepts.

Giacomo Balla intended that these three paintings should be hung together to form a triptych. He wished to portray three different moments of a speeding car penetrating the atmosphere. On the right, is his visual perception of a car speeding on a highway within a green landscape. In the center, the same "abstract speed lines" of the car are seen with the addition of zigzag lines indicating the noise produced by the roaring car. On the left, the speeding car and noise have passed and the highway remains in an empty landscape. The frames were painted by the artist.

4

"…..a roaring motor-car, which looks as though running on shrapnel, is more beautiful than the *Victory of Samothrace*."
INITIAL MANIFESTO OF FUTURISM
(February 20, 1909)

3

2

Triptych: (numbered from right to left).
2. *Abstract Speed* (1913). Oil on canvas, 19 3/4 x 25 3/4 inches. Collection Dr. W. Loeffler, Zurich. The abstract rendition of speed takes place in a landscape. The curved line representing the speed of the car is red; the vortex formed by the accelerated motion is pink; the sky is represented by the bluish curved lines that go from the top to the bottom of the painting; the road is white.
3. *Abstract Speed+Noise* (1913). Oil on canvas, 21 3/4 x 30 inches. Collection Peggy Guggenheim, Venice. The same landscape setting as in fig. 2 with additional blue and green criss-cross lines which indicate the noise of the speeding car.

4. *Abstract Speed - Wake of Speeding Automobile* (1913). Oil on canvas, 19 1/2 x 25 1/2 inches. Collection Marlborough Gallery, New York. The "line of speed," the "vortex of movement" and the angular "lines of noise" are absent. But curved lines seen in the two previous paintings representing the sky and the landscape remain. Other lines indicate the pink dust left by the car that has passed. Above the straight line on the left, representing the horizon, are green curved shapes representing trees in the landscape.

5. Aerial view, 1908, showing the Colosseum, the Roman Forum, and the Arch of Constantine. A series of photographs of archaeological sites in Italy were taken from a military balloon from 1904 to 1908. For the first time the Italian people had a bird's-eye view of their peninsula in a series of photographs taken from Mt. Etna to Trieste. In 1912, Marinetti, the Futurist poet, published in French a lyrical poem in free verse called "The Pope's Monoplane". In his "Technical Manifesto of Futurist Literature" published in Milan in 1912, Marinetti declared:

Profound intuitions of life, linked one to another, word to word, according to their illogical birth, will provide us with the general outlines of an intuitive psychology of matter. This flashed through my mind while I was up in an airplane. Looking at things from a new point of view, no longer from in front or from behind but from above — that is, in a foreshortened perspective — I was able to break the old shackles of logic and the plumb-lines of traditional comprehension.

5

6

7

8

9

6. Turin in the 1870's as Giacomo Balla saw it. He was born in the capital of Piedmont in 1871, near Piazza Vittorio Veneto (shown above left); both his parents were natives of Turin.
7. Balla at the age of five. His father, a chemist, died shortly afterwards.
8. Balla, second from right, at the age of 26, with friends in Turin. Previously he had worked for a commercial lithographer and had frequented night classes in drawing. It was his father's sister who suggested that he become a painter.

9. In 1895 he moved with his mother to Rome, where he lived for the rest of his life. He stayed for sometime in the Palazzo Quirinale with his uncle who was a game warden for King Umberto I. In Rome, Balla discovers the "magic Roman light." Irregular spaces and strong contrasts of meridional light and shade (as seen in this photograph of Piazza di Spagna about 1910) were strikingly different from the more rational spaces of Turin and the muted light of the northern atmosphere.

10

11

10. In his first Roman studio photographed about 1896. Balla is discernible in the lower center. His mother, a seamstress, is seated near the wall on which are hanging some of his early academic studies of the countryside around Rome.

11. A photograph today of his store-front studio which was located in Via Piemonte, near the Via Veneto. The painter Gino Severini identified the door to the right as the entrance to Balla's studio.

12

12. Balla at work out-of-doors about 1896. Like the Impressionists, he painted in "plein-air" in order to study light and color.

13

14

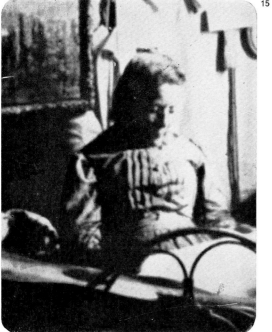

15

13. Photograph of Giacomo Balla, a few years after his arrival in Rome.

I consider the painter Giacomo Balla a typically Turinese genius. In fact, with the love of geometric order and the tenacious industry which are characteristic of the Piedmont capital, Balla organized and regimented his tumultuous creative energy. He was born in 1871, in Turin, of Turinese parents, on one of those great tree-lined boulevards which, opening in wide vistas onto the infinite, frame distant plains, hills and mountains with their dazzling glaciers, as if preparing for an artillery shot. These things taught him the plastic and spiritual value of space and kindled in his young muscles the urge to travel on land, on sea, and in the sky, following the most unbridled of fantasies.

(Marinetti)

16

17

18

14. Photograph of Elisa Marcucci, the Roman-born wife of the artist.

15. Photograph of Lucia Balla, the mother of the artist.

16. *Self-Portrait*. (1902). Oil on canvas, 22 3/4 x 17 3/4 inches. Collection Balla, Rome.

17. *Portrait of Elisa*. (1902). Pastel on paper, 16 5/8 x 21 1/4 inches. Collection Balla, Rome.

18. *Portrait of the Artist's Mother*. (1901). Pastel and tempera on paper, 47 x 36 1/2 inches. Collection Balla, Rome.

momento —

angolo della mia camera

valigia

19

20

19. In 1900, Balla spent seven months in France at Fontenay-Aux-Roses (near Paris), and drew this sketch of his room in a letter to his fiancée Elisa. On the floor near the door is his suitcase; above, on the wall, are sketches. On the right, a self-portrait and a pair of shoes.

20. Drawing for a large canvas entitled *The Path* (now lost) which was painted in Paris. In a letter to his fiancée Elisa, Balla wrote:

21

The portrait of that young lady is finished and it turned out well, only it will not interest the layman very much because the young lady is not very beautiful nor is she charming. The painting will be of interest to artists because I made a special study of the way the young lady walks *and I have succeeded in giv-*ing the illusion *that she is coming forward in a garden where one senses the presence of autumn.*

21. Tuscolo, a famous pilgrimage place because it is the site of an ancient Roman temple. Here, the artist (seated) was photographed with friends (1903) on one of his excursions to plant a tree. Every few years they carried a cypress, as much as 20 miles on foot, up the slopes of the Alban Hills to this hill top which has a magnificent, wide view of Rome and the countryside.

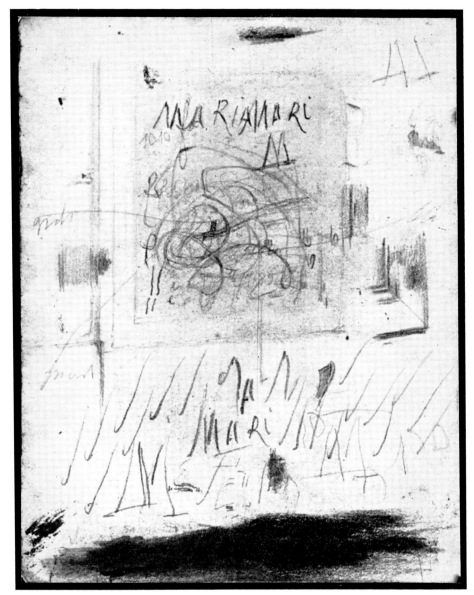

22

23

24

22. Drawing for *Bankrupt*. (1902). Pencil on paper, 3 7/8 x 3 1/8 inches. Collection Balla, Rome. This is a study for the upper part of the door on the left in that painting.

23. Detail of a "graffito" or actual wall-scribbling photographed about 1935 by Brassaï. (*Graffiti*, Paris, 1961).

24. Photograph of Balla pointing to a detail in his painting *Bankrupt*. (1902). Oil on canvas, 45 5/8 x 63 inches. Collection Cosmelli, Rome.

25

25. *Bankrupt.* (1962?). Oil on wood, 19 x 26 3/4 inches. Private collection, Rome. This painting on wood could be a study for the larger canvas painting. Balla selects the ordinary door of a store as the subject for his painting and "crops" the image as in a photograph. The doors of the bankrupt store were sealed by a court order. Children, oblivious of the human drama, awkwardly printed their names and scribbled numbers on it using blue chalk borrowed from a neighboring seamstress. Severini noted that "on a corner of the stone steps Balla has rendered spit magnificently."

26. Today the doorway, on the Via Veneto near the Porta Pinciana, has been replaced by the shop window of a bookstore.

26

27

29

28

27-28. Studies for *The Worker's Day*. (1904). Pencil on paper, 3 1/4 x 5 1/4 inches. Private collection, Rome.

29. Photograph of the building on the southeast corner of Via Salaria and Via Po, as it appears today. Balla painted this building in construction on the right-hand panel of *The Worker's Day*. The building that he used as the subject on the left-hand panels was on the site of number 19 Via Po, but has been replaced by a modern glass building.

30

30. *The Worker's Day.* (1904). Oil on paper,
39 1/2 x 53 1/8 inches. Collection Balla, Rome.
The painting is divided into three panels employ-
ing three different stages of light within one
day. On the upper left, the scaffolding is shown
in the early morning light. On the lower left,
the workman sit down to eat in the mid-day
sunlight. On the right, a group of workers, leaving for home at dusk, pass the softly illuminated sphere of a lamp-post while the light of the
evening is still reflected on the building's unfinished façade. The painted brick frame is by
Balla. The composition recreates and unites
three different moments in a simultaneous experience (space-time) in anticipation of the Futurist concept of simultaneity.

31

32

31. Balla playing "bocce" at a country restaurant near his home.

32. The artist inside his studio-apartment (1910) with his wife and daughter; standing is the sculptor Prini. Note the large pastel portrait of his mother on the wall.

33. Spadini, who lived nearby, painted *Balla's House* in 1922. Collection Pogliani, Rome. The upper left-hand story was Balla's studio-apartment in Via Paisiello which became the center of Futurist activity in Rome.

33

34. Aerial view, 1925, of Villa Borghese Park and the newly-built section of Rome, showing:
1) Balla's studio-home, an ex-monastery of the Frati della Vittoria dating from the 1700's. Balla lived here from 1904, when this zone was still countryside, until 1926 when the building was demolished to allow for the expansion of modern Rome.
2) Parco dei Daini (Deer Park). Site of his large Divisionist landscape painting (1910). See fig. 53.
3) A special area in Villa Borghese where Balla often worked out-of-doors. Day and night scenes of tree trunks, birds, and the sky as he saw them here were often the subjects for many of his paintings.
4) The southeast corner of Via Po and Via Salaria which is the site of the right-hand panel in *The Worker's Day* (1904). See fig. 30.
5) Piazza di Siena, the setting for *Patriotic Hymn* (1915). See fig. 147.

35. *Villa Medici* (1908). Oil on canvas, 38 1/2 x 54 inches. Private collection, Rome. Balla was a friend of a number of French art students as well as the Director of the French Academy in Villa Medici. This painting includes the portrait of one of his pupils, who is standing on a terrace overlooking the gardens of the villa.

36. A photograph taken sixty years later from the same terrace shows the extent of tree growth.

37

37. *Entrance to Palazzo Doria-Pamphili.* (1908). Pastel on paper, 17 3/4 x 22 1/2 inches. Private collection, Rome. Balla often stopped to look at doorways which were always full of mystery for him. Here he chose a perspective view seen in contrasting light.

38. Photograph of the same entrance, Palazzo Doria-Pamphili on the Via del Corso, Rome. Balla "frames" the doorway eliminating details of the façade.

38

▷

39. Overleaf: photograph taken about 1906 of a luncheon in Balla's studio against a background of his paintings. His wife Elisa, with their daughter Luce (blurred moving image), is at the head of the table. Right, Balla and three guests. Left, Countess Vimercati (who often posed for Balla), Grandmother Lucia (Balla's mother), Grandmother Gianna (Elisa's mother), and another guest. His early paintings are seen on the walls. Left to right: *The Beggar* (1902), *Elisa at the Door* (1904), *The Crazy Woman in Via Parioli* (lost), *The Water Carrier* (lost), and *The New Plane* (1903). Note the American flag (in honor of an American guest), the typical Roman country bread, and the flowers in the women's hair.

40-41. *Girl Looking at the Sea.* (1908). Oil on canvas, 19 1/4 x 23 1/2 inches. Private collection, Rome. On the back of this Divisionist painting is an unfinished painting of the sea executed at Anzio (fig. 41). Wavy irregular lines as on a transparent screen are superimposed on the sea, the clouds and the sky. These curly lines, that Balla perceives and portrays as brillant light are similar to the circular ones in the sky of *Parco dei Daini*. See fig. 46.

42. Balla at work on the terrace of Villa Sella overlooking the sea at Anzio. (1908).

43. Balla appearing as Jesus Christ in a "tableau vivant" photographed on the grounds of the Villa Sella at Anzio.

42

43

46

44. *Portrait of Ernesto Nathan.* (1910). Oil on canvas, 37 3/8 x 34 7/8 inches. Collection Galleria Comunale d'Arte Moderna, Rome (now hanging in the Campidoglio). The Mayor had no time to pose, so Balla studied him during working hours. The portrait was painted from memory in Balla's studio. Balla was a well-known and much appreciated portrait painter in Rome. 45. Ernesto Nathan, the Mayor of Rome, leaving the Quirinal after an official visit, in 1910. Nathan, a Socialist and anti-clerical, was mayor from 1907 to 1913. Born in London, he was fa-

mous for his honest and efficient administration at a time when Rome was rapidly expanding. 46. Detail of the *Parco dei Daini*, fig. 53. (1910). Oil on canvas, 30 1/4 x 43 inches. In a letter to Mr. Alfred H. Barr, Jr. in 1954 (additional text cf. Fig. 56), Balla wrote: *Painting light has always been my favorite theme. Besides particular studies, I have painted a large landscape (1910) in which I was able to represent the luminous vibration of the sky by means of blue, pink and mauve circular forms crossed by straight lines of pale yellow.*

47-52. Photographs taken recently in the Parco dei Daini (Deer Park), Rome. The park is located directly behind the Borghese Gallery in the Villa Borghese Park. Similar photographic angles reveal some of the objects in the painting: oversize statues, hanging branches of foliage, gravel on the ground, two stone pedestals, and the rear façade of the Borghese Gallery.

47-52

53

53. *Parco dei Daini.* (1910). Oil on canvas, 74 3/4 x 153 1/4 inches. Galleria d'Arte Moderna, Rome. Designed as a mural for a living room, Balla's concept of this composition, painted in the Divisionist technique, employed a loosely-constructed traditional perspective. However, Balla divided his architectural scheme for this large landscape into 15 panels. Then he took them one at a time out to the park, where he painted each one separately, standing at very different locations. The panels were subsequently assembled, and the actual landscape was re-organized according to Balla's pictorial purposes. Such an assemblage-composition suggests what was to become the Futurists' concept of simultaneity, of motion rendered as "space-time".

53 a. *Parco dei Daini.* (1910). Drawing on paper, 20 1/2 x 25 5/8 inches. Collection Balla, Rome. A study for the placement of the large landscape (fig. 53) in the decorative project designed by the artist for a living room.

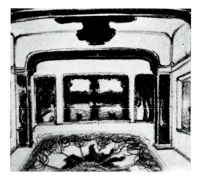

53a

54

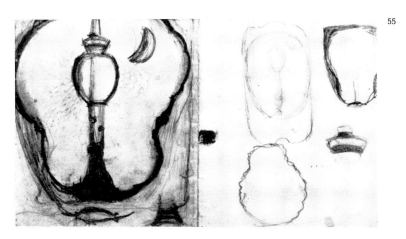

55

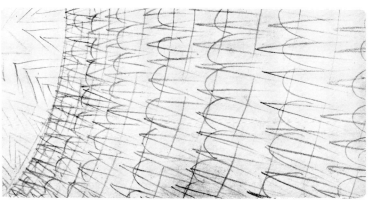

56

54. The old Stazione Termini (railroad station) in Rome.

55-56. Two studies for *The Street Light.* (1909). Both pencil on paper, 5 1/2 x 6 inches and 4 1/4 x 7 inches. The Museum of Modern Art, New York. The first study distinguishes the sphere of illumination from the area of darkness while, in the lower study, the chevron shapes interpenetrate with radiating circles.

Letter to Alfred H. Barr, Jr.

Rome, April 24th, 1954

Dear Mr. Barr:

I have received your letter of April the 9th; I am rather surprised at what you write. It is really absurd to doubt the authenticity of the date of one of my paintings, signed and dated by me, which comes from my studio. Here in Italy, everybody knows that my works are those of an innovator.

To give you a more precise example, let me explain that I painted the Lampada *in the Divisionist period (1900-1910). In fact, the glow of the light was obtained by means of combining pure colors.*

Besides being a very original work of art, it is also scientific because I sought to represent light by separating the colors which compose it. It is of great historical interest because of the technique and because of the subject.

No one in those days (1909) believed that an ordinary electric light could be the subject of a painting. On the contrary, I was inspired by it, and in the study, I wanted to represent light and, above all, to show that "romantic moonlight" had been supplanted by the light of a modern electric light bulb. In other words, I wanted to say that it was the end of Romanticism in art. It was my painting that inspired the phrase, "Let's kill the moonlight"....

The painting Lampada *was shown in Rome in one of the first Futurist exhibitions (1913) in the foyer of the Costanzi Theater. These early improvised exhibitions, put together with limited means, were very often lacking in catalogues, and, besides, I have always been very busy studying artistic problems and I never bothered to collect articles and catalogues.*

Concerning the installation of electric lights in Rome: the Technological Office of the Province, where I sought the information, states that those electric lights (BRUNT Model) were already in use in the principal streets of Rome in 1904, whereas in America and in England they still had not come into use.

The one I painted was in Piazza Termini...

G. Balla

57

58

57. Photograph of one of the 1904 Brunt arc lamps in Piazza Termini which was the subject of Balla's painting.

58. *The Street Light - Study of Light*. (1909). Oil on canvas, 68 3/4 x 45 1/4 inches. The Museum of Modern Art, New York. To study the forms and colors for this painting, Balla observed the light for hours on end, night after night. He went blind temporarily, and to regain his eyesight was forced to spend several days in a dark-ened room. The chevrons, radiating from the electric lamp, are painted in the colors of the spectrum. He later uses the same "rainbow" colors for his "Iridescent Interpenetration" studies (see figs. 67-80). Marinetti wrote the Futurist Manifesto "Let's Kill the Moonlight" in 1909; Balla, in his painting, has deliberately included the moon in the light sphere of the electric lamp as if to emphasize the triumph of electricity and progress.

59. Balla in motion, to suggest a sense of dynamism, in front of his painting *Dynamism of a Dog on Leash*. Photograph by Anton Giulio Bragaglia, first published in *Foto Dinamismo Futurista*, Rome, 1912. This book contained 16 photographs based on 16 different dynamic motions.
60. *Dynamism of a Dog on Leash*. (1912). Oil on canvas, 35 1/4 x 43 5/8 inches. Collection George F. Goodyear and the Buffalo Fine Arts Academy, New York. Painted in the summer of 1912 at Montepulciano, in the Chianti wine region, during a visit to one of his students. A swaying sparkling chain links the running dog to its owner who is walking. Balla uses a varied staccato technique in applying the paint in graduated brush strokes. The abstract "atmospheric" ground represents the white dust of the Tuscan countryside. When exhibited in 1912 in the Caffè Aragno in Rome, the public's reaction was violent, and several spectators struck the painting with their walking sticks.
61. This static image of a dachshund (Balla's dog model) emphasizes the dynamism of Balla's conception of a dog in motion.
62. Study for the painting *Dynamism of a Dog on Leash*. Pencil on paper, 3 x 5 1/8 inches. Notebook No. 4. Collection Balla, Rome.

60

61

62

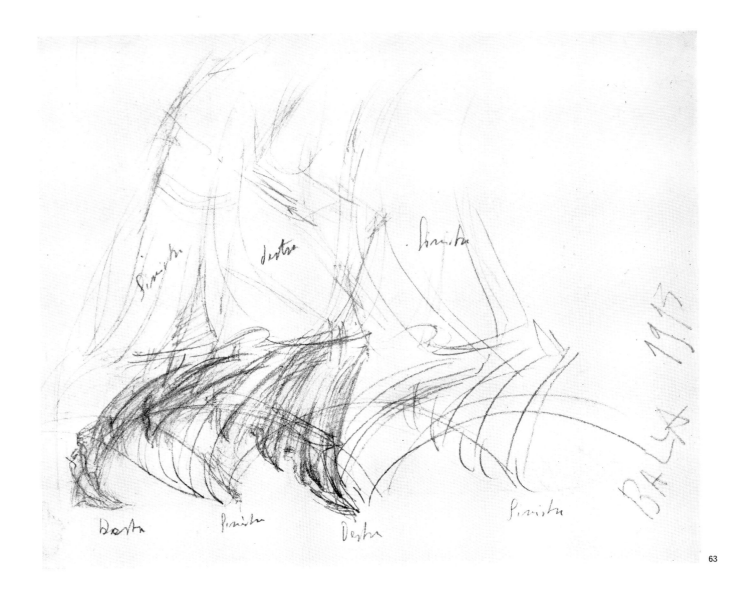

63

64

63. A study for *Girl Running on a Balcony*. (1912). Pencil on paper, 7 1/2 x 9 inches. Collection Abbate, Umbertide (Perugia). Balla has scribbled notations on the drawing of the "right-left" movements of the child's running feet and her figure in motion.

64. A photograph by Eadweard Muybridge of a girl running, selected from his eleven-volume work, *Animal Locomotion*, 1887. Muybridge's studies were made at the University of Pennsylvania. Each action was photographed in close sequence by three batteries of cameras.

65

66

65. *Portrait of Luce*. (1910). Oil on wood, 16 7/7 x 15 3/8 inches. Collection Balla, Rome. Balla's daughter, Luce (which means "light" in Italian), closely resembles her photograph in fig. 32.

66. *Girl Running on a Balcony* (1912). Oil on canvas, 49 1/4 x 49 1/4 inches. Civica Galleria d'Arte Moderna, Grassi Collection, Milan. From an open door inside his studio, Balla observed his daughter Luce running back and forth on the balcony outside. The air appeared to vibrate. Luce wore black boots and a blue linen dress; her pigtails were tied with blue ribbon. Her face and hands were pink, her hair brown. These vibrant colors and the dark railings of the balcony interpenetrate with the rhythmic left-right movements of the girl. The feeling of movement is heightened by the staccato technique with which the paint was applied. The pavement is a violet-gray. Balla always said (according to his daughters), "Use pure color — never mix."

67

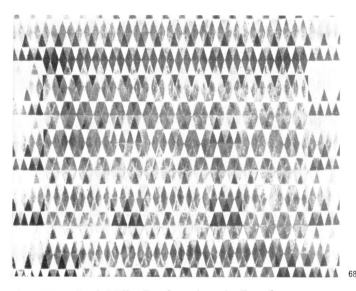

68

69

67. *Diptych of Villa Borghese.* (1905). Pastel on paper, each panel measures 10 1/4 x 13 3/4 inches. Collection Cosmelli, Rome. In the right-hand panel is the same eucalyptus tree which is visible behind the artist standing on his balcony in the photograph opposite (fig. 72).

68. *Iridescent Interpenetration No. 5. Eucalyptus.* (1914). Oil on canvas, 39 3/8 x 47 1/4 inches. Private collection, U.S.A. This rhythmic abstraction of shapes and colors in greens, yellows, and blues was inspired by the leaves of the eucalyptus tree behind his studio. In 1900, he even wrote from Paris asking for a eucalyptus leaf. M. Minnaert, in his book on *Light and Color* (p. 336) explains the appearance of green leaves under different light conditions: "A leaf on a tree is usually much more strongly illuminated on one side than on the other, and the color is essentially determined by whether we are looking at the side that is directly illuminated or the other side. In the former case, the light sent to us from the leaf is partly reflected at its surface, so that the colour becomes lighter but greyer. Moreover, when the leaf is illuminated from the front (relative to the observer), a bluish hue mingles with the green, and when from the back, a yellow hue."

69. *Iridescent Interpenetration No. 3.* (1912). Oil on canvas, 26 1/2 x 18 1/4 inches. Collection Marlborough Gallery, New York.

70

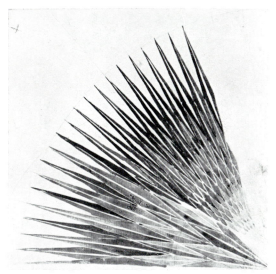

71

72

70. Photograph of eucalyptus leaves. Sunshine and the reflections on the leaves suggested the "iridescent interpenetration" which Balla translated into his studies of light and movement.
71. *Iridescent Interpenetration*. (Detail) 7 1/4 x 7 inches. Collection Balla, Rome. A study inspired by the eucalyptus leaves.
72. Balla on the balcony of his studio in Via Paisiello. Behind him is the large eucalyptus tree that he loved and constantly studied. From this same balcony, Balla observed his young daughter running as well as the swifts hovering around the corner of the rooftop which was also a subject for his paintings. Balla's view from his balcony looked out across Villa Bor-ghese to the dome of St. Peter's which could be seen in profile against the Roman sky.

73

74

73. Drawing of Balla, by Balla, in a Futurist suit which his wife made and which he wore in Dusseldorf where he had been invited by the Löwenstein family to design the décor for their house. Note the "Iridescent Interpenetration" tie.

74. A letter from Balla to his family from Düsseldorf, December 5th, 1912:

My dears,
First of all, enjoy this bit of rainbow: I am certain that you will like it. I have arrived at it after countless attempts and have at last found the meaning of delight in its simplicity. It will bring about other changes in my painting. The rainbow can, by a study of the real thing, give an infinite number of sensations of color. If I were not afraid of being mistaken, I should be finished in four or five days. I can see Mamma saying immediately: "Oh, well, he means twenty days or more; when he says that, you can be sure he means more." I know, mother dear, but it is not that way this time because the research is complete and everything is in order, and I don't intend to be disappointed. I am here in my cozy room, seated at this table with an electric light, a T-square, 2 boxes of paints, a telescope, a compass, a ceramic inkwell with flowers, a few books: Dante, Leonardo, Hugo...
(from the *Archivi del Futurismo*).

75 a-b. Two studies for *Iridescent Interpenetrations*. (1912-14). Watercolor on paper, 9 1/2 x 7 inches each. Collection Balla, Rome.

76 a-b. Two more studies for *Iridescent Interpenetrations*. (1912-14). Watercolor on paper, 8 5/8 x 7 inches each. Collection Balla, Rome.

75a-b

76a-b

77

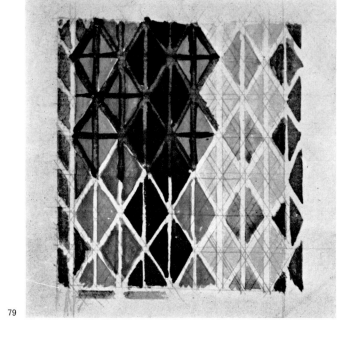

79

78

77-78-79. Studies of *Iridescent Interpenetration*.
(1912-13). Watercolor on paper, 4 1/4 x 4 inches,
8 5/8 x 7 inches, and 8 5/8 x 7 inches. Fig. 79.
Collection Civica d'Arte Moderna, Turin.
Figs. 77-78. Collection Balla, Rome.
80. *Iridescent Interpenetration No.* 9. (1912-13).
Oil on canvas, 16 7/8 x 20 7/8 inches. Collection
Balla, Rome. For the décor of the Löwenstein
house, situated on the Rhine (destroyed in World
War II), Balla made several projects as well as
a series of *Iridescent Interpenetrations*. Using the
same theme, he painted 6 oils on canvas, 3 on
paper and 3 on wood, as well as 6 temperas
and 1 water color. In the Dusseldorf notebook
there are 29 studies. (For the Manifesto "Seces-
sion," he made 14 studies, and there exist 20
various other studies.)

80

82

83

81

81. *The Typist*, a photograph by Anton Giulio Bragaglia, published in *Foto Dinamismo*, 1912. Bragaglia's early experiments in photodynamics took place in Rome around 1911-12, contemporary with the beginnings of the Futurist movement. He became an important figure in the cultural and artistic circles of Rome.

82-83. Two studies for *Rhythm of the Violinist*. (1912). Pencil on paper, each 3 1/4 x 4 inches. Galleria dell'Obelisco, Rome.

84

84. *Rhythm of the Violinist*. (1912). Oil on canvas, 20 1/2 x 2 91/2 inches. Collection Eric Estorik, on loan Tate Gallery, London. Painted in Düsseldorf, the hand is Mr. Löwenstein's, a lawyer and amateur violinist whose wife had been a pupil of Balla's. The trapezoidal shape of the canvas (within a rectangular frame) was also used by Balla in some of his studies of light and color (see figs. 74 and 80). It is interesting to compare the rendering of movement of the hand playing the violin with Bragaglia's photograph of the typing hands and to note that Balla studied the violin as a child.

85

86

Dir a tutti che il *critico d'arte passatista* è Benedetto Croce

87

88

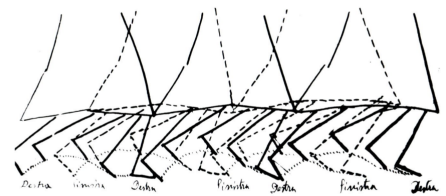

89

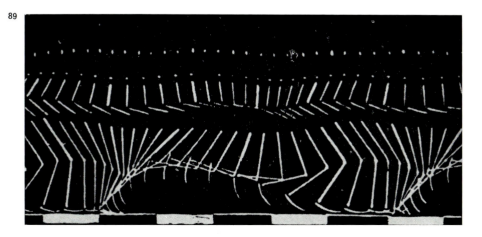

85. Photograph of a crowd looking at a Futurist painting. Luciano Folgore, the Futurist poet, has supplied this note as well as the photograph: "Rome, in the beginning of March, 1913, on Via delle Convertite, a short distance from the 'Terza Sala' of the Caffé Aragno which at that time was a meeting-place for the best-known writers, artists and journalists. There is a crowd in front of the show-window of the 'Lux' Bookstore, where a painting by Umberto Boccioni was on display, with a notice inviting the public to go see the exhibition of Futurist Painting which was then taking place in the Foyer of the Costanzi Theatre (now the Rome Opera House). The Lux Bookstore has been closed for many years."

86. A note in Balla's Notebook No. 4, about 1913: *Tell everyone that the old-fashioned art critic is Benedetto Croce*. Croce, the famous Neapolitan philosopher, was against the Futurists. Giovanni Papini delivered a lecture entitled "Against Rome and Against Benedetto Croce" at a Futurist meeting at the Teatro Costanzi on February 21, 1913. Balla and other Futurist painters were also on the stage.

87. A drawing in pencil on paper, 5 3/4 x 9 inches. (1912). Collection Balla, Rome. This study indicates the dynamic successive movements of a woman walking in various directions. (In Balla's time, women still wore long dresses).

88. Study for *Girl Running on a Balcony*. (1912). Ink on paper, 5 1/8 x 7 7/8 inches. Collection Balla, Rome. Balla is obsessed with the analysis of movement and distinguishes the rhythmic synchronization of left and right.

89. A photograph taken by Jules Marey shows the progress of a striding man dressed in black attire which has been marked by white dots and stripes (about 1882).

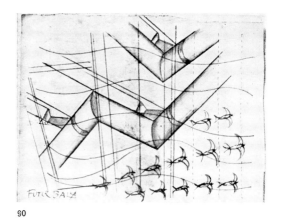

90

92

91

93. *Flight of Swifts.* (1913). Tempera on paper, 20 x 30 inches. Collection Nelson Rockefeller, New York. In the summer months great flights of swifts swoop around the roof-tops of Rome. Balla observed them for hours from his balcony. The white "coming and going" lines represent Balla himself going back and forth on the balcony, the "impalpable continuous motion." The angles of the drain-pipe and the slats of the shutters interpenetrate with the birds in flight and his "impalpable continuous motion." This was one of Balla's favorite expressions: *L'impalpabile andamentale.*

94. A Marey photograph. In 1882, the French scientist Jules Marey invented a "photo-gun" — a rudimentary type of movie camera. With it he was able to make 12 photographs per second of a bird in flight. This form of static, yet sequentially moving, photograph was the forerunner of the motion picture.

90. Study for *Swifts.* Ink on paper, 11 1/8 x 15 3/4 inches. Collection Balla, Rome. A preliminary study for his series of swifts in flight. Here he includes the same elements which he uses in his paintings: the drain-pipe, the Persian shutters, the swifts in flight, as well as the "coming and going" lines.

91. Study for *Swifts.* (1913). Watercolor on paper, 12 x 14 1/8 inches. Private collection, New York. A sense of motion is achieved by repeating and superimposing (as with photographic negatives) the stylized forms.

92. *Flight of Swifts.* (1913). Oil on canvas, 16 1/4 x 20 1/8 inches. Collection Marlborough Gallery, New York. The rhythmic staccato technique he uses in applying the paint in the background contrasts with the flowing movement of the birds in flight.

93

94

95

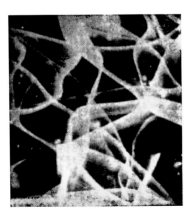

96

95. *Swifts: Paths of Movement + Dynamic Sequences.*
(1913). Oil on canvas, 38 x 47 1/4 inches. The
Museum of Modern Art, New York. Simultaneous movement in all directions is conveyed,
and from whatever point the spectator's eye
starts, it will be led throughout the composition. Here again the white lines, which Balla
intended to represent his movements on the balcony — that something intangible which is no
longer there — interpenetrate with the drain-
pipe, the Persian blinds and the swifts in flight.

We declare that the world's splendour has been enriched by a new beauty: the beauty of speed. A racing motorcar, its frame adorned with great pipes, like snakes with explosive breath... a roaring motorcar which looks as though running on shrapnel, is more beautiful than the Victory of Samothrace.
"Initial Manifesto of Futurism."
February 20, 1909.

Indeed, all things move, all things run, all things are rapidly changing. A profile is never motionless before our eyes, but it constantly appears and disappears. On account of the persistency of an image upon the retina, moving objects constantly multiply themselves: their form changes like rapid vibrations, in their mad career. Thus a running horse has not four legs but twenty, and their movements are triangular.
"Futurist Painting: Technical Manifesto,"
April 11, 1910.

97

96. Action photo taken with an open camera shutter from a bomber in a searchlight area. The film recorded broad waves which are the searchlights hunting for the moving plane. The total effect is the result of the combined movements of the lights and the diving of the bomber, simulating Balla's "impalpable continuous motion."

97. Balla was stimulated by the advent of the motorcar with its new possibilities for mobility and speed. The first Italian automobiles were produced in 1899 by the Fiat company in Turin. This is a Fiat type 3, 1910/1912.

98. Balla made this realistic sketch of the Fiat. (1909-10). Pencil on paper, 4 1/4 x 5 1/2 inches. Balla Collection, Rome. The model above closely resembles his drawing. He emphasized the chassis, the straight lines of the windscreen, and the wheels. From similar studies he developed his series on "abstract speed," based on direct observation of speeding cars. Balla, the pedestrian, made sketches of cars standing still, cars speeding by, wheels, vortexes, the density of atmosphere, and then, he interpreted all these sensations on the canvas in his studio.

98
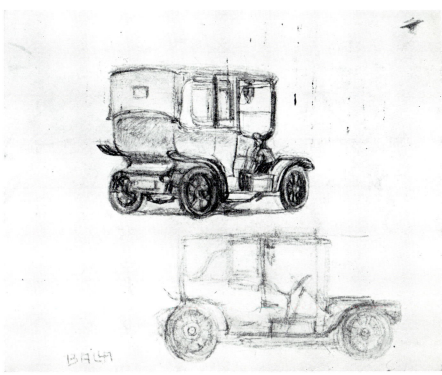

99

100

105

104

101

102

106

103

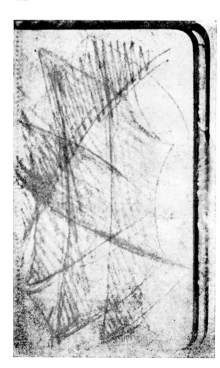

99-103. Studies of automobiles from Balla's Notebook No. 2. Pencil on paper, all 3 x 5 inches except fig. 102 which is 5 x 7 inches. Collection Balla, Rome. This is a series of drawings which Balla made in his notebook from direct observation of automobiles on the Roman streets. First he studied the car standing still, and then in motion. Balla was interested in speed for speed's sake. In fig. 101-103, the increasing speed of the car is pictorially represented by the progressive disappearance of its components so that in the last drawing (fig. 103), the car has almost disintegrated into an abstract representation of speed.

104. A photograph of the type of car, in this case the Fiat Type I, 1910-12, which Balla used as a model for the series of car studies shown here, as well as for the composition on the following page (fig. 107). Notice the folded down top of the convertible sedan in fig. 107.

105. *Vortex*. (c. 1913). Pencil on paper, 3 x 5 inches. Collection Balla, Rome. Notebook No. 2. One of many studies which Balla made of wheels in motion.

107

106. Study of the *Density of Atmosphere*. (c. 1913).
Pencil on paper, 3 x 5 inches. Collection Balla,
Rome. A study of atmosphere similar to the
one which the speeding car penetrates in the
painting on the right.

107. *Abstract Speed*. (1913). Tempera and ink on
paper, glued on canvas, 16 1/2 x 23 5/8 inches.
Private collection, Rome. The rotating tires of
the speeding car form a series of vortexes which
interpenetrate with the city street and the oblique lines that radiate from the steering wheel
and the wheels of the car. In the "Initial
Manifesto of Futurism," February 20, 1909,
the Futurists wrote: *We shall sing of the man
at the steering wheel, whose ideal stem trans-
fixes the Earth, rushing over the circuit of her
orbit*. The lines which form large projecting angles represent the atmosphere, and interpenetrate with the roof of the car, the protrud-
ing leather folds of the convertible top (note
fig. 101), and the arched doorways of a building
in Rome.

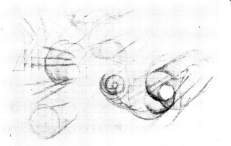

108

109

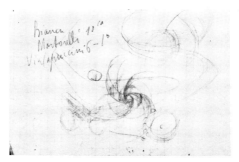

110

111

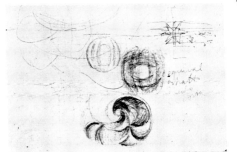

112

113

114

108-111. Studies of automobile wheels in movement taken from one of Balla's small pocket notebooks. Pencil on paper, 3 x 5 inches. Collection Balla, Rome. The wheel turning gradually faster and faster forms a whirling vortex.

112. An early Fiat Model. Type I. 1910-1912. Approximate speed was 20 to 30 miles per hour.

113. *The Car for Everyone*. (c. 1925). Tempera on paper, 23 1/4 x 17 3/4 inches. Collection Balla, Rome. An advertising poster designed by Balla for a garage.

114. *Study for Materiality of Lights + Speed* (1913). Gouache on paper, 11 3/4 x 17 inches. Collection Lydia Winston Malbin, Birmingham, Michigan. In this study of the night-reflections of a speeding car, Balla attempted to portray the effects of moving lights, moving wheels and simultaneous reflections. The wheels in movement produce a series of vortexes. The straight lines of the windshield interpenetrate with the curved lines of speed. The car is moving from left to right and the "space-time" intervals between the curved lines of speed expand indicating that the velocity of the car has increased.

115. *Abstract Speed.* (1913). Oil on canvas, 74 3/8 x 118 3/8 inches. Collection Balla, Rome. This large painting of speeding cars at night strongly resembles fig. 114. The repeated curved lines of speed produce space modulators as the car rips through the tangible space. The strong oblique lines emphasize the dynamic force behind the lines of speed. Here the driver is partially visible in the contrasting light. Speed had become the subject of visual analysis and Balla attempted to render motion (space-time) on a static plane. Note that in each of Balla's studies of speeding cars, the car is speeding from right to left but, as the spectator's eye is accustomed to reading images from left to right, the sense of speed is accentuated.

116. *Speeding Automobile.* (1912). Oil on wood, 21 7/8 x 27 7/8 inches. The Museum of Modern Art, New York. Reflected in a large glass window of a store front are refracted light images of a car seen speeding past at night. In the upper center there is the reflected image of a small round light in front of the store that radiatet larger areas of flickering colors, such as lighs green, red, violet, etc. The decomposition of the car's expanding form as it penetrates the atmosphere can be seen in the reflections of the store window.

117. *Environmental Drawing for a Speeding Automobile.* (1912). Pencil on paper, 5 1/4 x 7 inches. Collection Balla, Rome. The store front and colors of the reflected light images are noted in this study for the above painting (Fig. 116).

116

117

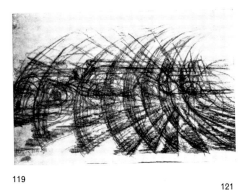

118   119   121

120

122

118. Study for *Noise Forms of a Motorcycle*. (1916). Pencil on paper, 4 x 6 inches. Collection Balla, Rome.

119. Study for *Noise Forms of a Motorcycle*. (1916). Enamel on paper, 26 3/4 x 38 inches. Collection Balla, Rome. Straight horizontal lines represent the *"l'impalpabile andamentale,"* translatable as the "impalpable continuous motion," which, in this case, is actually the trail of the speeding motorcyclist's body. These are interwoven with vortexes (produced by the speeding wheels), with curved lines of speed, and with diagonal lines radiating from the handle bars.

120. An early motorcycle, vintage 1909, manufactured by the Moto-Gilera Company in Milan.

121. A sidecar with a motorcycle, manufactured in England, 1914. (Courtesy *Motor Cycle*, London).

122. *Noise Forms of a Motorcycle*. (1916). Oil on paper, 27 1/4 x 39 3/8 inches. Collection Raimondo Bariatti, Milan. Painted after a ride in the sidecar of a friend's motorcycle, this is Balla's visual perception of his new experience. The angular forms and zigzags represent strident sound waves produced by the speeding motorcycle, while the smooth intertwined spiral stands for the "line of speed." Curved forms on the lower left represent the sidecar. The spinning rear wheel, the motorcycle chain and part of a fender are distinguishable. Large angular volumes represent backfire.

123. *Vortex + Spatial Forces of a Glass*. (1911-13). Tempera on paper, 7 1/4 x 4 1/4 inches. Collection Walter Pharr, New York. According to Balla's daughters, this tempera deals with an object of classical still-life painting. He gives it the same dynamic qualities which characterize his painting of motorcycles or speeding cars

126

124

125

124. *Airplanes.* (1915-18). Tempera on cardboard, 5 1/4 x 5 7/8 inches. Collection Balla, Rome. Two airplanes (Caproni biplanes), flying against a contrasting pale and darker blue sky, produce large diagonal airwaves in the patriotic colors of red, white and green.

125. A Caproni airplane in flight, Model CA 33,450 Horsepower. Gianni Caproni, an engineer, was a pioneer in designing and constructing airplanes in Italy. This was the first large-scale bomber produced and it was used in the First World War. It was also manufactured in England, France and in the United States by the Curtis Company. (Photo credit: Aeronautical Museum of Caproni di Taliedo, Rome).

126. This postage stamp issued in Italy in 1968 reproduces the tempera (fig. 124) of airplanes by Balla next to a portrait of Francesco Baracca (not by Balla). This stamp was to commemorate the 50th Anniversary of the death in action of Francesco Baracca, the Italian aviation ace of the First World War.

127-28. Two studies of a propeller in motion. Tempera on paper, each 9 3/4 x 8 inches. (c. 1913) Collection Balla, Rome.

129. The propeller of a Caproni monoplane of 1913. Balla chose the name Elica (Propeller) for his second daughter. (Photo credit: Aeronautical Museum of Caproni di Taliedo, Rome).

130. A drawing of Balla's ballet *Dance of the Propeller* reproduced from the newspaper *L'Impero*, 1927. Pencil on paper, 12 x 16 1/2 inches. Collection Balla, Rome. The dancers, holding propellers in both hands, are seen on a vertical stage set. They seem to be flying in the sky represented by two curved lines as is often seen in Balla's paintings (see Figs. 2, 3 and 4). The caption under the reproduction reads: "A Painting in Movement by G. Balla."

127

128

130

L'IMPERO — Pagina num. 3 — Venerdì 14 Ottobre 1927

Un quadro in movimento di G. Balla

129

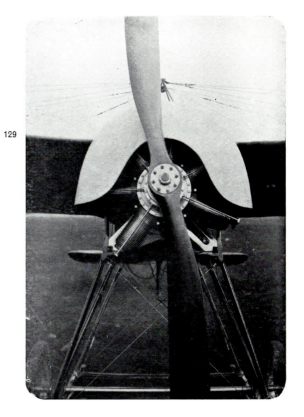

FUTUR BALL Tra la giovane sposina la vecchia vedova la fonte perenne cantava....

" La Cinna.... di S. PASCOLI.

131. *Study* for *Blue Orbits*. (1913). Blue pencil on paper, 18 7/8 x 25 1/4 inches. Private collection, Rome. The blue interpenetrating circles suggest celestial orbits as well as the round shape of a telescope whose slight movements are superimposed. Again note the curving lines, from top to bottom, representing the sky.

132. Balla's telescope. He was an enthusiastic amateur astronomer.

133. *Mercury Passing before the Sun as seen through a Telescope*. (1914). Tempera on paper, 47 1/4 x 39 inches. Collection Gianni Mattioli, Milan.

Mercury, in the upper center, is seen as a tiny circle. Slightly lower is a much larger orange circle representing the sun. The phenomenon which took place on November 7th, 1914 was not visible to the unaided eye. Balla observed the eclipse with his telescope and a dark glass filter which perhaps suggested to him the burnt brown, yellow, orange and violet colors used in the painting. The glaring white image to the left of Mercury is the eclipse as it appeared to Balla's naked eye when the telescope slipped slightly from his eyesight.

132

133

134

136

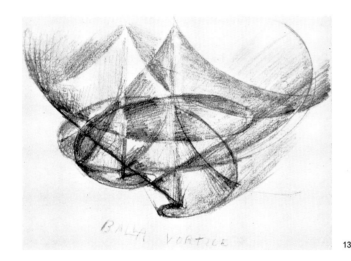

135

137

135a

138

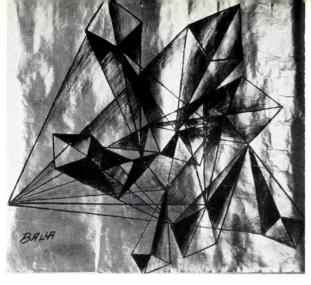

140

140a

141

134. Photograph showing the vortexes created by objects moving in space. Mobile entitled *Virtual Volume* by William Matson (1914) published by Moholy-Nagy (p. 237, fig. 322).

135-135a. Two studies both entitled *Vortex*. (1914). Pencil on paper, 15 1/4 x 6 7/8 inches. Coll. Balla, Rome. In fig. 135, Balla interpenetrates the forms of two vortexes; in fig. 135a, he defines the vortex by means of repeated linear outlining of space.

136. Reconstruction (1968) of the original *Line of Speed + Vortex* (1913-14). Wire sculpture, 32 inches high and 46 inches wide. Collection Joseph H. Hirschhorn, Greenwich, Connecticut.

137. *Line of Speed + Vortex*. (1913-14). Working drawing for the wire sculpture in fig. 136, as seen from above. Watercolor in red and blue on paper, 13 3/8 x 19 1/4 inches. Coll. Balla, Rome.

138. *Line of Speed + Vortex*. (1913-14). A scale drawing of the frontal view of the sculpture, fig. 136. Watercolor in red and blue on paper, 13 1/4 x 17 1/4 inches. Collection Balla, Rome.

139. *Noise Forms*. (1913-14). Enamel on gold paper, 13 3/8 x 14 1/4 inches. Collection Irene Brin, Rome. The gold paper gives the further sensation of crackling noises.

140. *Noise Forms*. (1914-15). Pencil on paper, 4 1/2 x 7 1/4 inches. Collection Balla, Rome. Balla uses these studies in many of his later paintings, such as the speeding motorcycle, and in the painted tapestries.

140 a. *Noise Forms*. (1914-15). Pencil on paper, 4 1/2 x 6 1/4 inches. Collection Balla, Rome.

141. *Expansion of Perfume*. (c. 1918). Pastel on paper, 6 1/4 x 8 5/8 inches. Collection Balla, Rome. Balla's visual interpretation of perfume penetrating the air.

IL VESTITO ANTINEUTRALE

(THE ANTI-NEUTRAL SUIT)

We glorify war, the only hygiene for the world.
Marinetti (Ist Futurist Manifesto - February 20, 1909)

Long live Asinari di Bernezzo!
Marinetti. (Ist Futurist Soirée - Teatro Lirico, Milan, February, 1910)

Humanity has always dressed *quietly*, with *fear*, with *caution* or with *indecision*. It has always worn mourning, cape and cloak. Man's body has always been diminished by *neutral* shades and tones, degraded by black, suffocated by belts and imprisoned by drapery.

Up to the present, men have used clothes with static shapes and colors, in other words, draped, solemn, grave, uncomfortable and priestly. They were expressions of timidity, melancholy and *slavery*; they were negations of the body's muscular activity, which was suffocating beneath an unhygienic tradition of materials which were too heavy and of tedious, effeminate and decadent half-tints. Tonalities and rhythms of a *distressing* peace, funereal and depressing.

Today we want to abolish:

1. All *neutral*, "nice," faded, *fancy*, dull and humiliating colors.

2. All pedantic colors and styles, all those which are professorial and teutonic. All striped, checkered and *diplomatic dot* patterns.

3. All mourning clothes, not even suitable for grave-diggers. Heroic deaths should not be mourned, but remembered with scarlet clothes.

4. The equilibrium of the mediocre, the so-called good taste, and the so-called harmony of colors and shapes which restrain enthusiasm and slow down the pace.

5. Symmetrical tailoring, *static* lines which tire, depress, sadden and bind the muscles; the uniformity of clumsy lapels and all the excessive trimmings. Useless buttons, starched collars and cuffs.

We Futurists want to free our race from every form of *neutrality*, from frightened and silent indecision, from negating pessimism and from nostalgic romantic, mollifying inertia. We want to color Italy with Futurist audacity and danger, and at long last, give the Italians agressive and cheerful clothes.

Therefore Futurist clothes will be:

1. *Aggressive*, so aggressive as to increase the courage of the brave and shock the sensitivity of cowards.

2. *Stream-lined*, so as to increase the suppleness of the body and favor the impetus of fighting, running and charging.

3. *Dynamic*, thru the patterns and colors of the materials (triangles, cones, spirals, ellipses, circles) inspiring love of danger, of speed, and of attack, and hate of peace and immobility.

4. *Simple and comfortable*, that is, easy to put on and take off, well-suited for aiming a rifle, fording rivers, and swimming vigorously.

5. *Hygienic*, that is, cut in such a manner that every part of your skin can breathe on long walks or tiring ascents.

6. *Joyous*. Materials in exciting colors and iridescences. Use *muscular* colors, the brightest violets, reds, turquoises, greens, yellows, oranges, scarlets.

7. *Luminous*. Phosphorescent materials which can stir up boldness in a timid assembly, spread light around when it rains, and counterbalance the grayness of the twilight in the streets and on our nerves.

8. *Strong-willed*. Violent patterns and colors, imperious and impetuous like orders shouted on a battlefield.

9. *Asymmetrical*. For example, the ends of sleeves and the fronts of jackets should be round on the right and square on the left. Spirited counterattacks of lines.

10. *Of short duration*, so as to constantly renew the pleasure and the impetuous animation of the body.

11. *Variable*, by means of « modifiers » (cloth trimmings of different size, thickness, color and pattern). These may be applied whenever and wherever one wishes, on whatever part of the dress one wishes, by means of metallic snaps. In this way, anyone can create a new outfit on the spur of the moment. The modifier shall be arrogant, vexing, clashing, decisive, warlike, etc. The Futurist hat shall be asymmetrical and in gay, aggressive colors. Futurist shoes shall be dynamic, each one different in form as well as color, and easily suitable for kicking all the neutralists.

IL VESTITO ANTINEUTRALE

Manifesto futurista

Glorifichiamo la guerra, sola igiene del mondo.
MARINETTI.
(1° Manifesto del Futurismo - 20 Febbraio 1909)

Viva Asinari di Bernezzo!
MARINETTI.
(1° Serata futurista - Teatro Lirico, Milano, Febbraio 1910)

L'umanità si vestì sempre di **quiete**, di **paura**, di **cautela** o d'**indecisione**, portò sempre il lutto, o il piviale, o il mantello. Il corpo dell'uomo fu sempre diminuito da sfumature e da tinte **neutre,** avvilito dal nero, soffocato da cinture, imprigionato da panneggiamenti.

Fino ad oggi gli uomini usarono abiti di colori e forme statiche, cioè drappeggiati, solenni, gravi, incomodi e sacerdotali. Erano espressioni di timidezza, di malinconia e di **schiavitù,** negazione della vita muscolare, che soffocava in un passatismo anti-igienico di stoffe troppo pesanti e di mezze tinte tediose, effeminate o decadenti. Tonalità e ritmi di **pace desolante,** funeraria e deprimente.

OGGI vogliamo abolire:

1. — Tutte le tinte **neutre,** « carine », sbiadite, *fantasia*, semioscure e umilianti.

2. — Tutte le tinte e le foggie pedanti, professorali e teutoniche. I disegni a righe, a quadretti, a **puntini diplomatici.**

3. — I vestiti da lutto, nemmeno adatti per i becchini. Le morti eroiche non devono essere compiante, ma ricordate con vestiti rossi.

4. — L'equilibrio **mediocrista,** il cosidetto buon gusto e la cosidetta armonia di tinte e di forme, che frenano gli entusiasmi e rallentano il passo.

5. — La simmetria nel taglio, le linee **statiche,** che stancano, deprimono, contristano, legano i muscoli; l'uniformità di goffi risvolti e tutte le cincischiature. I bottoni inutili. I colletti e i polsini inamidati.

Noi futuristi vogliamo liberare la nostra razza da ogni **neutralità,** dall'indecisione paurosa e quietista, dal pessimismo negatore e dall'inerzia

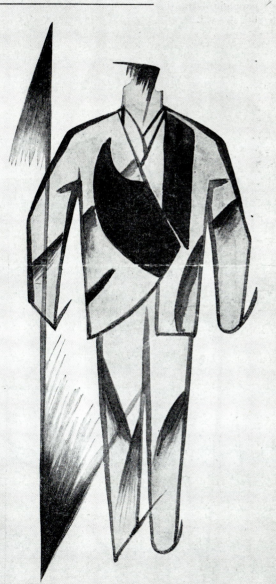

Vestito bianco - rosso - verde del parolibero futurista Marinetti. *(Mattino)*

nostalgica, romantica e rammollente. Noi vogliamo colorare l'Italia di audacia e di rischio futurista, dare finalmente agl'italiani degli abiti bellicosi e giocondi.

Gli abiti futuristi saranno dunque:

1. — **Aggressivi,** tali da moltiplicare il coraggio dei forti e da sconvolgere la sensibilità dei vili.

2. — **Agilizzanti,** cioè tali da aumentare la flessuosità del corpo e da favorirne lo slancio nella lotta, nel passo di corsa o di carica.

3. — **Dinamici,** pei disegni e i colori dinamici delle stoffe, (triangoli, coni, spirali, ellissi, circoli) che ispirino l'amore del pericolo, della velocità e dell'assalto, l'odio della pace e dell'immobilità.

4. — **Semplici e comodi,** cioè facili a mettersi e a togliersi, che ben si prestino per puntare il fucile, guadare i fiumi e lanciarsi a nuoto.

5. — **Igienici,** cioè tagliati in modo che ogni punto della pelle possa respirare nelle lunghe marcie e nelle salite faticose.

6. — **Gioiosi.** Stoffe di colori e iridescenze entusiasmanti. Impiegare i colori *muscolari*, violettissimi, rossissimi, turchinissimi, verdissimi, gialloni, aranciooooni, vermiglioni.

7. — **Illuminanti.** Stoffe fosforescenti, che possono accendere la temerità in un'assemblea di paurosi, spandere luce intorno quando piove, e correggere il grigiore del crepuscolo nelle vie e nei nervi.

8. — **Volitivi.** Disegni e colori violenti, imperiosi e impetuosi come comandi sul campo di battaglia.

9. — **Asimmetrici.** Per esempio, l'estremità delle maniche e il davanti della giacca saranno a destra rotondi, a sinistra quadrati. Geniali controattacchi di linee.

10. — **Di breve durata,** per rinnovare incessantemente il godimento e l'animazione irruente del corpo.

11. — **Variabili,** per mezzo dei **modificanti** (applicazioni di stoffa, di ampiezza, spessori, disegni e colori diversi) da disporre quando si voglia e dove si voglia, su qualsiasi punto del vestito, mediante bottoni pneumatici. Ognuno può così inventare ad ogni momento un nuovo vestito. Il modificante sarà prepotente, urtante, stonante, decisivo, guerresco, ecc.

Il cappello futurista sarà asimmetrico e di colori aggressivi e festosi. Le scarpe futuriste saranno dinamiche, diverse l'una dall'altra, per forma e per colore, atte a prendere allegramente a calci tutti i neutralisti.

Sarà brutalmente esclusa l'unione del giallo col nero.

Si pensa e si agisce come si veste. Poichè **la neutralità è la sintesi di tutti i**

Vestito bianco - rosso - bleu
del parolibero futurista Cangiullo. *(Pomeriggio)*

passatismi, noi futuristi sbandieriamo oggi questi vestiti antineutrali, cioè festosamente bellicosi.

Soltanto i podagrosi ci disapproveranno.

Tutta la gioventù italiana riconoscerà in noi, che li portiamo, le sue viventi bandiere futuriste per la nostra grande guerra, **necessaria, URGENTE.**

Se il Governo non deporrà il suo vestito passatista di paura e d'indecisione, noi **raddoppieremo, CENTUPLICHEREMO IL ROSSO** del tricolore che vestiamo.

MILANO, 11 Settembre 1914.

Giacomo Balla

pittore.

Approvato entusiasticamente dalla Direzione del Movimento futurista e da tutti i Gruppi Futuristi italiani.

Modificanti guerreschi e festosi.

STAB. TIP. TAVEGGIA - MILANO VIA OSPEDALE 3

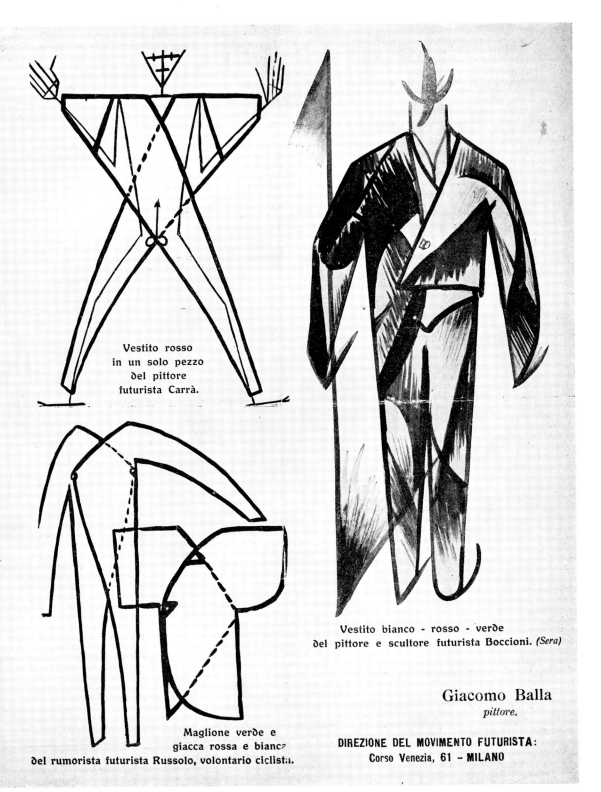

Vestito rosso
in un solo pezzo
del pittore
futurista Carrà.

Vestito bianco - rosso - verde
del pittore e scultore futurista Boccioni. *(Sera)*

Maglione verde e
giacca rossa e bianca
del rumorista futurista Russolo, volontario ciclista.

Giacomo Balla
pittore.

DIREZIONE DEL MOVIMENTO FUTURISTA:
Corso Venezia, 61 – MILANO

The combination of yellow and black will be brutally excluded.

One thinks and one acts as one dresses. Since *neutrality is the synthesis of all traditional ideas*, we Futurists are now displaying these anti-neutral suits which are so joyfully aggressive.

Only the old fogies shall disapprove.

All Italian youth shall recognize in us, who wear them, its living Futurist flags for our great war, which is *necessary* and *URGENT*.

If the Government does not discard its traditional clothes of fear and indecision, we shall *double*, we shall *MULTIPLY BY A HUNDRED THE RED* of the tricolor flag which we wear.

GIACOMO BALLA, Painter
Milan, September 11th, 1914.

Translation of illustrations of ANTI-NEUTRAL SUIT MANIFESTO:

142. Red-white-green suit of the Futurist "*parolibero*" [free-word poet] Marinetti. (Morning).
143. Red-white-blue suit of the Futurist "*parolibero*" Cangiullo. (Afternoon).
144. Warlike and festive modifiers.
145. One-piece red suit of the Futurist painter Carrà.
145 a. Green sweater, and red and white jacket of the Futurist "*rumorista*" [noise-maker] Russolo, voluntary cyclist.
145 b. Red-white-green suit of the Futurist painter and sculptor Boccioni. (Evening).

146

147

146. *Patriotic Hymn*. (1915). Oil on canvas, 43 1/4 x 65 inches. Collection Balla, Rome. This painting was inspired by a public demonstration in the Piazza di Siena (open arena) in the gardens of the Villa Borghese. Interventionists had called for Italy to renounce her alliance with Germany and to intervene in the war on the side of England and France. The towering rectangular forms which are painted in red, white and green — the colors of the Italian flag — represent the patriotic hymns sung by children at the rally. A beam of golden sunlight enters from the upper right corner of the painting.

147. Aerial view (1925) of the Piazza di Siena in Villa Borghese, Rome. The elliptical form of the arena is clearly represented in the painting above.

149

148. Detail of a photograph of the Monument to Victor Emanuel II in the Piazza Venezia, Rome. The photograph was taken from a dirigible in 1917. (Photo credit: Aeronautical Museum of Caproni di Taliedo, Rome). The monument contains the Tomb of the Unknown Soldier and is referred to as the "Altar of the Country." Inaugurated in 1911, the national shrine was designed by Giuseppe Sacchi and, in the eyes of Balla and the Italian people, it represented the unity of Italy.

149. *Flags on the Altar of the Country.* (1915). Oil on canvas, 39 3/8 x 39 3/8 inches. Collection Benedetta Marinetti, Rome, In front of Balla's abstracted image of the Victor Emanuel II monument are groups of Italian flags and a large, encompassing curved form suggesting the noise of the Interventionist demonstration held in favor of Italian participation in the First World War. The predominance of dark blue-gray colors suggest that the day was overcast. The Futurists declared: "We wish to glorify War — the only hygiene for the world — militarism, patriotism, the destructive arm of the Anarchist, the beautiful Ideas that kill, the contempt for woman." (Article 9, from the "Initial Manifesto of Futurism," February 20, 1909).

148

150

151

152

150. *Shouting Forms — Long Live Italy*. (1915). Oil on canvas, 52 3/4 x 74 inches. Collection Balla, Rome. This painting is a visual record of the sensations which the artist experienced at a demonstration in the Piazza del Quirinale, in front of the Palazzo, then the King's palace. Balla participated in all the patriotic demonstrations of 1915 with great enthusiasm. The two large, wave-like, swelling volumes represent the shouting of patriotic slogans and the small swirling volumes stand for crowds of men in straw boaters. Visible in the upper center is an owl-like form with a knotted rope, which is the insignia of the House of Savoy.

151. Photograph taken in 1915 during a demonstration in the same square, Piazza del Quirinale.

152. Detail of a photograph of the Piazza del Quirinale taken from a dirigible in 1917. (Photo credit: Aeronautical Museum of Caproni di Taliedo, Rome).

BALLA

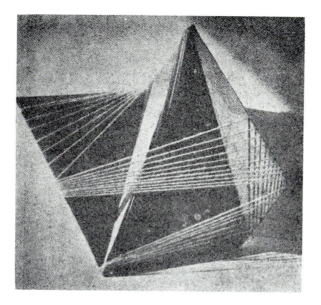

N. 3. **Complesso plastico colorato di linee-forze**

(Cartone, lana, filo rosso, filo giallo)

DEPERO

N. 5. **Complesso plastico colorato motorumorista simultaneo di scomposizione a strati**

DEPERO

N. 4. **Complesso plastico colorato**

(Latte e carte colorate)

DEPERO

N. 6. **Complesso plastico colorato motorumorista di equivalenti in moto**

(Veli colorati, cartoni, stagnole, fili metallici, legno, tubi, pulegge)

DIREZIONE DEL MOVIMENTO FUTURISTA - Corso Venezia, 61 - MILANO

specchi, làmine metalliche, stagnole colorate, e tutte le sostanze sgargiantissime. Congegni meccanici, elettrotecnici; musicali e rumoristi; liquidi chimicamente luminosi di colorazione variabile; molle; leve; tubi, ecc. Con questi mezzi noi costruiamo dei

ROTAZIONI

1. *Complessi plastici che girano su un perno* (orizzontale, verticale, obliquo).
2. *Complessi plastici che girano su più perni*: *a*) in sensi *uguali*, con velocità varie; *b*) in sensi *contrarî*; *c*) in sensi *uguali e contrarî*.

SCOMPOSIZIONI

3. *Complessi plastici che si scompongono*: *a*) a volumi; *b*) a strati; *c*) a trasformazioni successive in forma di coni, piramidi, sfere, ecc.).
4. *Complessi plastici che si scompongono, parlano, rumoreggiano, suonano simultaneamente.*

SCOMPOSIZIONE
TRASFORMAZIONE
} FORMA + ESPANSIONE {
ONOMATOPEE
SUONI
RUMORI

MIRACOLO
MAGIA

5. *Complessi plastici che appaiono e scompaiono*: *a*) lentamente; *b*) a scatti ripetuti (a scala); *c*) a scoppi improvvisi.

Pirotecnica — Acque — Fuoco — Fumi.

La scoperta-invenzione sistematica infinita

mediante l'astrattismo complesso costruttivo rumorista, cioè lo stile futurista. Ogni azione che si sviluppa nello spazio, ogni emozione vissuta, sarà per noi intuizione di una scoperta.

ESEMPI: Nel veder salire velocemente un aeroplano, mentre una banda suonava in piazza, abbiamo intuito il **Concerto plastico-motorumorista nello spazio** e il **Lancio di concerti aerei** al di sopra della città. — La necessità di variare ambiente spessissimo e lo sport ci fanno intuire il **Vestito trasformabile** (applicazioni meccaniche, sorprese, trucchi, sparizioni d'individui) — La simultaneità di velocità e rumori ci fa intuire la **Fontana giroplastica rumorista**. — L'aver lacerato e gettato nel cortile un libro, ci fa intuire la **Réclame fono-moto-plastica** e le **Gare pirotecnico-plastico-astratte**. — Un giardino primaverile sotto il vento ci fa intuire il **Fiore magico trasformabile motorumorista**. — Le nuvole volanti nella tempesta ci fanno intuire l'**Edificio di stile rumorista trasformabile**.

Il giocattolo futurista

Nei giochi e nei giocattoli, come in tutte le manifestazioni passatiste, non c'è che grottesca imitazione, timidezza, (trenini, carrozzini, pupazzi immobili, caricature cretine d'oggetti domestici), *antiginnastici o monotoni, solamente atti a istupidire e ad avvilire il bambino.*

Per mezzo di complessi plastici noi costruiremo dei giocattoli che abitueranno il bambino:

1) *a ridere apertissimamente* (per effetto di trucchi esageratamente buffi);

2) *all'elasticità massima* (senza ricorrere a lanci di proiettili, frustate, punture improvvise, ecc.);

3) *allo slancio immaginativo* (mediante giocattoli fantastici da vedere con lenti; cassettine da aprirsi di notte, da cui scoppieranno meraviglie pirotecniche; congegni in trasformazione ecc.);

4) *a tendere infinitamente e ad agilizzare la sensibilità* (nel dominio sconfinato dei rumori, odori, colori, più intensi, più acuti, più eccitanti).

5) *al coraggio fisico, alla lotta e alla* **GUERRA** (mediante giocattoli enormi che agiranno all'aperto, pericolosi, aggressivi).

Il giocattolo futurista sarà utilissimo anche all'àdulto, poichè lo manterrà *giovane, agile, festante, disinvolto, pronto a tutto, instancabile, istintivo e intuitivo.*

RICOSTRUZIONE FUTURISTA DELL'UNIVERSO

Col Manifesto tecnico della Pittura futurista e colla prefazione al Catalogo dell'Esposizione futurista di Parigi (firmati Boccioni, Carrà, Russolo, Balla, Severini), col Manifesto della Scultura futurista (firmato Boccioni), col Manifesto La Pittura dei suoni rumori e odori (firmato Carrà), col volume *Pittura e scultura futuriste*, di Boccioni, e col volume *Guerrapittura*, di Carrà, il futurismo pittorico si è svolto, in 6 anni, quale superamento e solidificazione dell'impressionismo, dinamismo plastico e plasmazione dell'atmosfera, compenetrazione di piani e stati d'animo. La valutazione lirica dell'universo, mediante le Parole in libertà di Marinetti, e l'Arte dei Rumori di Russolo, si fondono col dinamismo plastico per dare l'espressione dinamica, simultanea, plastica, rumoristica della vibrazione universale.

Noi futuristi, Balla e Depero, vogliamo realizzare questa fusione totale per ricostruire l'universo rallegrandolo, cioè ricreandolo integralmente. Daremo scheletro e carne all'invisibile, all'impalpabile, all'imponderabile, all'impercettibile. Troveremo degli equivalenti astratti di tutte le forme e di tutti gli elementi dell'universo, poi li combineremo insieme, secondo i capricci della nostra ispirazione, per formare dei complessi plastici che metteremo in moto.

Balla cominciò collo studiare la velocità delle automobili, ne scoprì le leggi e le linee-forze essenziali. Dopo più di 20 quadri sulla medesima ricerca, comprese che il piano unico della tela non permetteva di dare in profondità il volume dinamico della velocità. Balla sentì la necessità di costruire con fili di ferro, piani di cartone, stoffe e carte veline, ecc., il primo complesso plastico dinamico.

1. Astratto. — **2. Dinamico**. Moto relativo (cinematografo) + moto assoluto. — **3. Trasparentissimo**. Per la velocità e per la volatilità del complesso plastico, che deve apparire e scomparire, leggerissimo e impalpabile. — **4. Coloratissimo** e **Luminosissimo** (mediante lampade interne). — **5. Autonomo**, cioè somigliante solo a sè stesso. — **6. Trasformabile**. — **7. Drammatico**. — **8. Volatile**. — **9. Odoroso**. — **10. Rumoreggiante**. Rumorismo plastico simultaneo coll'espressione plastica. — **11. Scoppiante**, apparizione e scomparsa simultanee a scoppî.

Il parolibero Marinetti, al quale noi mostrammo i nostri primi complessi plastici ci disse con entusiasmo: « L'arte, prima di noi, fu ricordo, rievocazione angosciosa di un Oggetto perduto « (felicità, amore, paesaggio) perciò nostalgia, statica, dolore, lontananza. Col Futurismo invece, l'arte « diventa arte-azione, cioè volontà, ottimismo, aggressione, possesso, penetrazione, gioia, realtà bru- « tale nell'arte (Es.: onomatopee. — Es.: intonarumori = motori), splendore geometrico delle forze, « proiezione in avanti. Dunque l'arte diventa Presenza, nuovo Oggetto, nuova realtà creata cogli « elementi astratti dell'universo. Le mani dell'artista passatista soffrivano per l'Oggetto perduto; « le nostre mani spasimavano per un nuovo Oggetto da creare. Ecco perchè il nuovo Oggetto « (complesso plastico) appare miracolosamente fra le vostre. »

La costruzione materiale del complesso plastico

MEZZI NECESSARI: Fili metallici, di cotone, lana, seta, d'ogni spessore, colorati. Vetri colorati, carteveline, celluloidi, reti metalliche, trasparenti d'ogni genere, coloratissimi. tessuti,

THE FUTURIST RECONSTRUCTION OF THE UNIVERSE

G. Balla, F. Depero

March 11th, 1915

The Technical Manifesto of Futurist Painting, the foreward to the Catalogue of the Futurist Exhibition in Paris (signed by Boccioni, Carrà, Russolo, Balla, Severini), the Manifesto of Futurist Sculpture (signed by Boccioni), the Manifesto of the Painting of Sounds, Noises and Odors (signed by Carrà), the volume *Pittura e scultura futuriste* (Futurist Painting and Sculpture) by Boccioni, and Carrà's book *Guerrapittura* (War-painting) mark the development of Futurist painting over the past six years, surpassing and solidifying Impressionism, plastic dynamism and moulding of atmosphere, interpenetration of planes, and states of mind. The lyrical evaluation of the universe, as expressed by the Free Words of Marinetti, and Russolo's Art of Noises, blend together with plastic dynamism to give the dynamic, simultaneous, plastic and noisy expression of the universal vibration.

We Futurists, Balla and Depero, wish to carry out this total fusion in order to reconstruct the Universe by bringing it joy, that is, by recreating it completely. We shall give flesh and bones to the invisible, the impalpable, the imponderable, the imperceptible. We shall find the abstract equivalents of all the forms and of all the elements of the universe, and then we shall combine them according to the whims of our inspiration in order to form plastic constructions [*complessi plastici*] which we shall then put into motion.

Balla began by studying the velocity of automobiles; this led him to discover its laws and essential linear-forces. After more than twenty paintings in the same research, he realized that the flat surface of the canvas did not permit him to render in depth the dynamic volume of speed. Balla felt the need to build — using wire, pieces of cardboard, cloth and tissue-paper, etc. — the first dynamic plastic construction [*complesso plastico*].

1. *Abstract*. - 2. *Dynamic*. Relative motion (cinema) + absolute motion. - 3. *Very Transparent*. Because of the speed and the volatility of the plastic construction which should appear and disappear, very light and impalpable. 4. *Very Colorful* and *Very Luminous* (by means of internal lights). - 5. *Autonomous*, that is, only resembling itself. - 6. *Transformable*. - 7. *Dramatic*. - 8. *Volatile*. -

9. *Odorous*. - 10. *Noisy*. Plastic noise simultaneous with plastic expression. - 11. *Exploding*, appears and disappears simultaneously accompanied by explosion. The free-word poet [*parolibero*] Marinetti, to whom we showed our first plastic constructions, said to us with enthusiasm: "Before us, art was memory, the anguished evocation of a lost Object (happiness, love, landscape) and therefore nostalgic, static, painful and remote. With Futurism, on the other hand, art becomes art-action, that is, willfulness, optimism, aggression, possession, penetration, joy, brutal reality in art (e.g.: onomatopoeia. e.g.: tuned noises = motors), geometric splendor of energy, a foreward thrust. Therefore, art becomes a Presence, a new Object, a new reality created with the abstract elements of the universe. The hands of the traditional artist pined for the lost Object; our hands long for a new Object to be created. That is why the new Object (plastic construction [*complesso plastico*] appears miraculously in your hands.

The material construction of the plastic construction [complesso plastico]
Necessary Material: Wire, cotton, colored wool and silk threads of all thicknesses. Colored glass, tissue-paper, celluloid, metal screens, all sorts of very colorful transparencies. Fabrics, mirrors, metal sheets, colored tin-foil and all sorts of very gaudy substances. Mechanical, electrical, musical and noise-making devices; chemically luminous liquids of variable coloration; springs, levers, tubes, etc. With this material we put together:

ROTATIONS
1. Plastic constructions which rotate on a pivot (horizontal, vertical, oblique).
2. Plastic constructions which rotate on several pivots: a) in the same direction but with different speeds; b) in opposite directions; c) in same and opposite directions.

DECOMPOSITIONS
3. Plastic constructions which break up into: a) volumes; b) strata; c) successive transformations in the form of cones, pyramids, spheres, etc.
4. Plastic constructions which break up, speak, make noise and play music simultaneously.

DECOMPOSITION TRANSFORMATION	FORM + EXPANSION	ONOMATOPEIA SOUNDS NOISES

Il paesaggio artificiale

Sviluppando la prima sintesi della velocità dell'automobile, Balla è giunto al primo complesso plastico (*N. 1*). Questo ci ha rivelato un paesaggio astratto a coni, piramidi, poliedri, spirali di monti, fiumi, luci, ombre. Dunque un'analogia profonda esiste fra le linee-forze essenziali della velocità e le linee-forze essenziali d'un paesaggio. Siamo scesi nell'essenza profonda dell'universo, e padroneggiamo gli elementi. Giungeremo così, a costruire

l'animale metallico

Fusione di arte + scienza. Chimica, fisica, pirotecnica continua improvvisa, dell'essere nuovo automaticamente parlante, gridante, danzante. Noi futuristi, Balla e Depero, costruiremo milioni di animali metallici, per la più grande guerra (conflagrazione di tutte le forze creatrici dell'Europa, dell'Asia, dell'Africa e dell'America, che seguirà indubbiamente l'attuale meravigliosa piccola conflagrazione umana).

Le invenzioni contenute in questo manifesto sono creazioni assolute, integralmente generate dal Futurismo italiano. Nessun artista di Francia, di Russia, d'Inghilterra o di Germania intuì prima di noi qualche cosa di simile o di analogo. Soltanto il genio italiano, cioè il genio più costruttore e più architetto, poteva intuire il complesso plastico astratto. Con questo, il Futurismo ha determinato il suo Stile, che dominerà inevitabilmente su molti secoli di sensibilità.

MILANO, 11 Marzo 1915.

Balla
Depero
astrattisti futuristi

BALLA

N. 1. **Complesso plastico colorato di frastuono + velocità**
(Cartone e stagnole colorate)

BALLA

N. 2. **Complesso plastico colorato di frastuono + danza + allegria**
(Specchi, stagnole, talco, cartone, filferro)

DIREZIONE DEL MOVIMENTO FUTURISTA: Corso Venezia, 61 - MILANO

153

154

153. *The 20th of September Demonstration.* (1915).
Oil on canvas, 29 1/4 x 39 3/8 inches. Collection
Balla, Rome. An idealized abstraction of a demonstration, held at the Porta Pia on September
20, 1915, in favor of Italian participation in the
First World War. September 20th was an important Italian national holiday commemorating
the capture of papal Rome by the Bersagliere
troops in 1870. The moving red shapes stand
for the red shirts of the "Garibaldini" — veter-
ans of Garibaldi's campaign. The hovering
green shapes at the top represent the trees
along the Roman wall at Porta Pia.

154. A photograph of 1870 of the Roman
Wall at Porta Pia, showing the breach made by
the Italian national troops on September 20,
1870, and the location of the Interventionist
demonstration held in 1915.

MIRACLE MAGIC

5. Plastic constructions which appear and disappear: a) slowly; b) by repeated jerky movements (on scale); c) in sudden explosions. Fireworks - Water - Fire - Smoke.

The infinite systematic discovery-invention
by means of complex, constructive, noise-making abstraction, namely, the Futurist style. Every action which takes place in space, every emotion experienced, shall be for us the intuition of a discovery. *Examples*: Watching an airplane climbing rapidly while a band played in the square, we had the intuition for the PLASTIC MOTOR-NOISE CONCERT IN SPACE and the LAUNCH OF AIR CONCERTS over the city. - The need to change environment frequently and our love of sports gives us the idea for the TRANSFORMABLE SUIT (mechanical applications, surprises, tricks, disappearing people). - The simultaneity of speed and noises inspires the REVOLVING-PLASTIC NOISE-MAKING FOUNTAIN. Tearing up a book and throwing it down into the courtyard, gives us the idea for PHONO-MOVING PLASTIC ADVERTISEMENTS and PYROTECHNIC - PLASTIC - ABSTRACT - CONTESTS. A spring garden in the wind inspires the MAGIC TRANSFORMABLE MOTOR-NOISE-MAKING FLOWER. - Clouds scurrying in a storm give us the idea for the TRANSFORMABLE NOISE-MAKING STYLE OF BUILDING.

THE FUTURIST TOY
In games and toys, as in all traditional manifestations, we find only grotesque imitations and timidity (little trains, little carriages, motionless dolls, idiotic caricatures of domestic objects). All these are unathletic and boring, only capable of making the child more stupid and more degraded. Using plastic constructions [*complessi plastici*], we shall devise toys that shall accustom the child to:
1. *laughing heartily* (a consequence of exaggeratedly funny tricks);
2. *the maximum agility* (without resort to throwing projectiles, whippings, sudden stings, etc.);
3. *an imaginative impetus* (by means of fantastic toys to be seen through lenses; boxes, to be opened at night, from which beautiful fireworks will explode; transforming mechanisms, etc.);
4. *extend infinitely and sharpen the senses* (in the boundless domain of noises, odors, colors, ever more intense, more acute and more stimulating).
5. *physical courage for fighting and for WAR* (by means of huge outdoor toys, dangerous and aggressive).

The Futurists toy shall also be very useful to adults, since it shall keep them *young*, *agile*, *gay*, *unself-conscious*, *ready for everything*, *tireless*, *instinctive and intuitive*.

THE ARTIFICIAL LANDSCAPE
Developing the first synthesis of the speeding automobile, Balla arrived at the first plastic construction (No. 1). This revealed to us an abstract landscape consisting of cones, pyramids, polyhedrons, spirals of mountains, rivers, lights, shadows. There exists a profound analogy between the essential linear-forces of speed and the essential linear-forces of a landscape. We have delved into the profound essence of the universe, and now we control the elements. We shall thus be able to build...

THE METAL ANIMAL
Fusion of art + science. Chemistry, physics, continuous unexpected pyrotechnics of a new creature that speaks, shouts and dances automatically. We Futurists, Balla and Depero, shall construct millions of metal animals for the greatest war (a conflict between all the creative forces of Europe, Asia, Africa, and America), which will undoubtedly follow the present marvelous little human conflagration.

All the inventions contained in this Manifesto are total creations, generated in full by Italian Futurism. No artist in France, Russia, England or Germany ever conceived anything similar or analogous before we did. Only the Italian genius, namely the most constructive and architectural genius, could have conceived the abstract plastic construction [*complesso plastico astratto*]. With this, Futurism has defined its style which shall inevitably dominate many centuries of sensitivity.
Milan, March 11th, 1915   BALLA DEPERO
Futurist abstractionists

TRANSLATED CAPTIONS of illustrations in "THE FUTURIST RECONSTRUCTION OF THE UNIVERSE":
No. 1 - (Balla) Colored plastic construction of noise + speed. (Colored cardboard and tinfoil).
No. 2 - (Balla) Colored plastic construction of noise + dance + merriment. (Mirrors, tinfoil, talc, cardboard, wire).
No. 3 - (Balla) Colored plastic construction of linear-forces (Cardboard, wool, red thread, yellow thread).
No. 4 - (Depero) Colored plastic construction (Tins and colored paper).

155. The Marchesa Luisa Casati. A photograph of the international social celebrity and eccentric, famous for her hats and dresses. A friend of the avant-garde painters and writers, she was also an idol of D'Annunzio, Diaghilev and the Ballet Russe.

156. *The Marchesa Casati with Greyhound and Parrot*. (1915). Ink on paper, 11 x 8 inches. Collection Balla, Rome.

157. *The Marchesa Casati*. (1915). A portrait bust in painted wood and cardboard. Present whereabouts unknown; formerly in Collection Marinetti. Her smile is represented by the two fluted forms on either side, which were a strong pink. The convoluted forms at the top were copper color and stood for her hair. Above the right eye is the representation of the black moleskin plaster which the Marchesa was in the habit of wearing in place of eyebrows. The black mica eyes of the sculpture were placed on a pivot linked to a kind of "line of speed in volume" which also suggests a heart. The "heart," when turned by the spectator's hand, made the eyes blink. The Marchesa's face is very pale white, the eyes are outlined in black and the mouth is a brilliant red. Various colors behind the puctured holes changed when the "heart" was turned.

155

156

No. 5 - (Depero) Simultaneous noise-making, colored plastic construction, decomposable into strata.

No. 6 - (Depero) Noise-making, colored plastic construction made up of moving equivalents. (Colored veils, cardboard, tinfoil, metal wires, wood, pipes, pulleys).

157

158

160

159

161

FUTURISMO Il Futurismo, religione di orgoglio italiano, velocità, originalità, eroismo, amore del pericolo, ottimismo artificiale, sport e forza muscolare, guerra, pugno-argomento, arte-vita, splendore geometrico, estetica della macchina, parole in libertà, dinamismo plastico, architettura pura, teatro sintetico simultaneo, vita simultanea, tattilismo, arte dei rumori, nacque nel febbraio 1909 a Milano e rinnovò il mondo.

MARCIARE NON MARCHRE

Il Futurismo, minoranza d' artisti creatori, esige qualità non quantità, pochi ma originali. Ogni città contiene ingegneri audaci. Bisogna riunirli in gruppo, e rispettando la loro indipendenza, costringerli ad un minimo di solidarietà novatrice. Essenziale, la passione per l'Italia e per il nuovo. Il Futurismo, movimento ideologico artistico letterario scientifico interviene nella politica soltanto quando la Patria pericola. I Futuristi uniti da questa vigilanza e pronti a tutto, appoggiano ciò che è originale ed eccentrico e colorano le città col loro temperamento italiano acceso.

MOVIMENTO FUTURISTA
diretto da
F. T. MARINETTI
Piazza Adriana, 30
ROMA (33)

IL PUGNO DI BOCCIONI

F. T. MARINETTI

158. A photograph of Umberto Boccioni, one of the major exponents of Futurism, holding a palette.

159. *Boccioni's Fist - Lines of Force.* (1915). Wood and cardboard sculpture painted red, 33 x 28 3/4 inches. Collection Lydia Winston Malbin, Birmingham, Michigan.

This sculpture synthesizes the Futurist assault on everything belonging to the past. The dynamic image produced by the interpenetration of geometric forms represents the forces emanating from the moving figure of Boccioni and his fist in tension. It illustrates most successfully Balla's prescription for the material conception of the *complesso plastico* (plastic construction) under the category of Decompositions in the "Futurist Manifesto: Reconstruction of the Universe" (March 11, 1915).

162

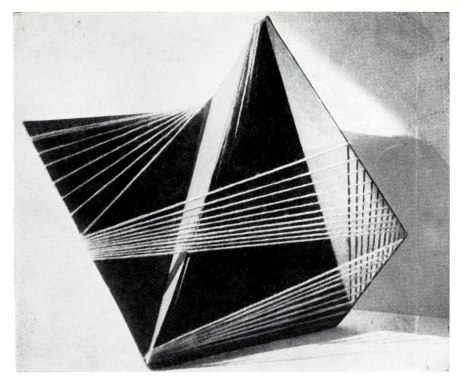

163

164

160. A drawing for the sculpture *Boccioni's Fist*. (c. 1914-15). Pencil on paper, 16 7/8 x 8 1/4 inches. Collection Balla, Rome. The past is represented as an old bearded man in front of ancient columns and arches. The letters "Futurista" are written over the lines of force of Boccioni's body which are dynamically threatening these symbols of tradition.

161. Another drawing for the same sculpture which later became the letter-head for Futurism used by Tomaso Marinetti, the Futurist poet.

162. *"Complesso Plastico" colored fo Noise + Dance + Happiness*. (1914-15). Original photograph. Plastic construction made of mirrors, tin-foil, talcum powder, cardboard, and wire. Now destroyed, it was published in the manifesto "Futurist Reconstruction of the Universe" (1915).

163. *"Complesso Plastico" colored of lines + forces*. (1914-15). Plastic construction made of cardboard, wool, red and yellow string. 11 3/4 x 15 3/4 x 6 1/4 inches. Original photograph 1914-15. With the "complesso plastico," the Futurists tried to redirect traditional concepts of art.

164. *"Complesso plastico" of noise + speed*. (1914-15). Original made with cardboard and colored tin-foil. Reconstruction (1968) cast in aluminum and steel. 32 x 46 inches. Collection Joseph H. Hirschohrn, Greenwich, Connecticut.

164

164. *Study for the set of the Stravinsky-Diaghilev ballet Fireworks.* (1916-17). Tempera on paper, 19 1/8 x 13 inches. Collection Balla, Rome. The ballet was performed on April 12th, 1917 at the Teatro Costanzi, the opera house of Rome. Balla, seeking to interpret the music in terms of color and form, constructed the set in cloth and transparent paper using beams of light to indicate the musical rhythms. A battery of lights, controlled by Balla stationed in the prompter's box, produced 76 different combinations of lights. The light program ranged from flooding the theater with light to plunging it into total darkness. The performance lasted 4 minutes and 4 seconds, the exact duration of Stravinsky's music. No dancers appeared on the stage, for the great innovation of the ballet was its abstract character. It was not well received by the Roman audience as a whole, but the few who approved of Balla's genius clamored for him to appear. He ran onto the stage in his Futurist suit, brandishing a purple straw hat in one hand and a square-cut walking stick in the other, and exclaiming "Benone!! Benone!" (Fine!! Fine!).
165-172. In 1968, Elio Marchegiani, using Balla's notes and scale drawings, skillfully reconstructed a model of the ballet set for Stravinsky's "Fireworks". On the opposite page are photographs of six of the 76 electronically-programmed light changes.
The reconstruction is on the scale of 1:13,333, approximately the size of a large television set; the Stravinsky music was taped and coordinated with the lights.

 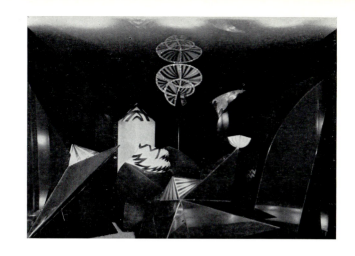

 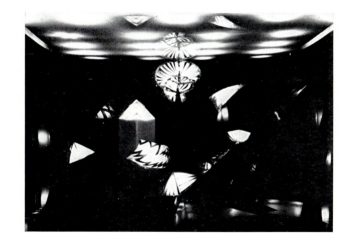

 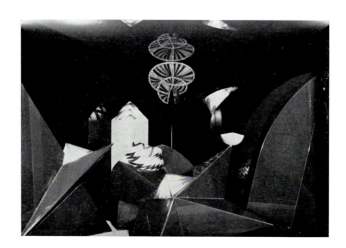

173

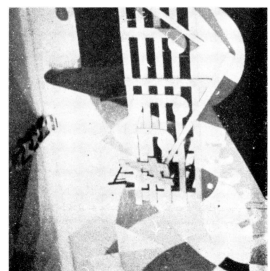

174

173. Balla designed the furniture, murals and décor for the Bal-Tik-Tak, the first modern nightclub in Rome. This is a sketch for the Futurist electric street sign (20 feet long) designed by Balla for the Bal-Tik-Tak. It was forcefully removed the first night by the Rome Fire Department because it was considered to be too glaring.

175

176

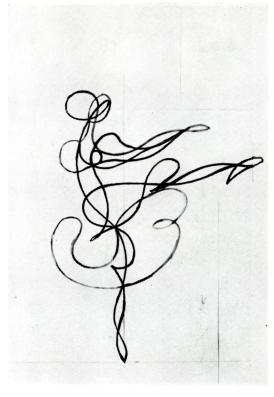

177

178

179

174. The building which housed the Bal-Tik-Tak in Via Milano as it appears today.
175. One of Balla's ceiling decorations for the Bal-Tik-Tak.
176. The musicians' balcony at the Bal-Tik-Tak designed by Balla.
177-78. Balla designed and executed five murals of dancers using five different steps: *Ecarté*, *Pas des Deux*, *Danse du Feu*, *Duo*, and *Serpentina*. Designs for two of the murals for the Bal-Tik-Tak, *Ecarté* and *Duo* (1920), are shown here. Fig. 177 is blue ink on paper, 20 5/8 x 17 3/4 inches. Fig. 178 is blue and red ink on paper, 25 1/4 x 16 1/2 inches.
179. *Pas des Deux*. (1922). Wire sculpture, height 20 inches. Balla executed in 1922 a series of wire sculptures based on the murals of dancers for the Bal-Tik-Tak. Photograph of a "reconstruction from the original" made in 1968; collection Joseph H. Hirschhorn, Greenwich, Connecticut.

180

180. *Transformation of Forms into Spirits.* (1920). Tempera on paper, 11 3/8 x 11 1/4 inches. Collection Balla, Rome. One of a series of paintings on a mediumistic theme. On the lower left, the curved dark horizon of the earth emanates violet prismatic forms which represent spirits. To the right of the intense blue sky are cosmic rays which are represented by thick white oblique lines. The cosmic rays nuture the "spirit" forms which are transformed in the upper left into curved green forms.

181. Photograph, taken by the Gemini 4 spacecraft during its June 3-7 orbital mission, shows the earth's curved horizon with a view of clouds over the ocean, looking towards the sun (1965).

181

182. A poster Balla designed in 1918, using *Boccioni's Fist* as a theme, for his one-man exhibition at the *Casa d'Arte Bragaglia*. In 1928, Virgilio Marchi, the Futurist architect, wrote in his retrospective article on Balla: *Anyone who would have wanted to see the new Futurist, no longer a very young man, fight for the new ideals, should have gone to see the exhibition that took place when Bragaglia still had his gallery on Via Condotti and where Balla also gave a brillant lecture, well-spiced with free-word-plays, good humor, studied elegance and an intelligent contradictory discussion. All the brightest lights of the avant-garde were present at those memorable afternoon gatherings.*
Virgilio Marchi, *La Stirpe*, 1928

On the following page is the Manifesto which was included in the exhibition catalogue of 1918.

182

MANIFESTO OF COLOR

1. Given the existence of photography and of the cinema, pictorial reproduction of reality does not and cannot interest anyone.

2. In the turmoil of avant-garde tendencies, whether they are semi-Futurist or Futurist, color dominates. Color must dominate because it is the typical privilege of the Italian genius.

3. Impotence of color and the cultural heaviness of all Nordic painting eternally shrouds art, in gray, in mourning, in passivity, in monkishness, in stiffness, in pessimism, in neutrality, and in effeminate graciousness and indecision.

4. Futurist Italian painting is, and must be always more explosive in color, and cannot be other than playful, daring, etherial, electrically cleansed, dynamic, violent and interventionist.

5. All traditional or pseudo-Futurist paintings give a sensation of staleness, of being old, tired, and already digested.

6. Futurist painting is a painting of combustion, a painting of surprises.

7. Dynamic painting: simultaneity of forces.

183

183. For the decoration of the « Teatro degli Indipendenti » in via degli Avignonesi, 1921-22, the old vaulting was covered with burlap and Balla painted a luminous and multi-colored transparent ceiling. Directed by Giulio Anton Bragaglia, author of *Fotodinamismo*, the theater was housed amidst the ruins of the Baths of Settimo Severio beneath the Palazzo Vittoni.

184

185

186

187

184. *Tennis + Landscape*. (1920). Oil on canvas, 26 x 57 1/4 inches. Collection Slifka, New York. This view of Villa Borghese from Balla's balcony shows a tennis player in action; the path of the ball can be traced to the lower left.

185. *Futurist Blackbirds*. (1920). Oil on canvas, 26 x 57 1/2 inches. Collection Balla, Rome. Another subject painted from Balla's balcony shows quarrelling blackbirds whose noises are represented by zigzag crossing curved lines. Here, the movement, the sound, the space have been transformed into a two-dimensional color composition.

186. *Futurist Flower*. (1920). Oil on canvas, 39 3/8 x 57 1/2 inches. Collection Campilli, Rome. In this realistic painting of an actual Futurist environment of Balla's own creation, a three-dimensional stylized flower, constructed of wood and painted in bright colors, stands on a table.

187. Photograph of Balla with his daughters Luce and Elica, holding a larger version of the wooden flower construction (c. 1929) which is the subject of the painting in fig. 186. At his feet are small versions of other flowers from the "Futurist garden." Balla's Futurist jacket is black, lemon, yellow and turquoise blue.

188

189

188. Paper studies for Futurist sculptures. These constructions are three-dimensional multiple-plane conceptions made of flat cut-outs niched together and polychromed. Some of these asymmetrical shapes were inspired by actual flowers and as sculpture, they were meant to represent flowers. Others are more utilitarian in design, such as the table supported by the cut-out figure of a man (center). In the right background is a construction of the number 2.

189. This small floral form, measuring approximately 13 inches high and 9 inches wide, was one of the original series (1918-1930) of painted wooden sculptures constructed of flat units inserted into each other, easily mantled and dismantled. The basic units were of relatively simple shapes, and thus could be easily manufactured in quantity as Balla's intention was that Futurist sculpture would be readily available to the public. The emphatic stylized forms used in some of the flowers are similar to the dynamic "lines of force" in his paintings.

190

191

190. Another flower from the small series of polychromed wood constructions (1918-1930) measuring approximately 13 inches high.

191. A photograph taken by Jannelli, the journalist, about 1931, of Balla in his Futurist suit, holding a Futurist Flower (fig. 189). On the table of his studio is *Boccioni's Fist* and material for making sculptures. The painting *Perhaps* is hanging in the upper background; leaning against the table is his painting *Futurist Blackbirds* (fig. 185).

192. *The Spell is Broken.* (1924-5). Oil on canvas, 42 1/4 x 30 1/4 inches. Collection Balla, Rome. A metaphysical painting in which Balla seeks to translate a state of being into shapes and color. The effect of a broken spell on what was a charmed experience is portrayed by the gray boomerang shapes breaking up the composition of the word *"incanto"* (enchantment), which can be deciphered in the canvas. The individual letters vary greatly in size and are painted as three-dimensional forms. The color tones range from white to pale pink, and to a brillant shocking-pink.

193. *Pessimism and Optimism.* (1923). Oil on canvas, 17 1/2 x 23 1/2 inches. Private collection, Rome. Symbolizing the forces of good and evil at work in the universe, this painting was considered by Balla to be the summation of Futurist visual ideals. In abstract terms, it expresses his theories concerning line, space and interpenetration, in perfect equilibrium. Evil forces are painted black (the absence of light), angular, hostile, prismatic, and irregular in rhythm. Good forces are blue, regular in rhythm and wheeling continually to ward off the insidious attacks of evil.

193

After the war, predictably and yet miraculously, his masterpiece finally appears: 'Optimism and Pessimism'. Any Italian, who has not yet fathomed the achievements and the infinite possibilities of Futurist painting, can profit by studying the funereal pointed tentacles of traditional Pessimism which will certainly be overcome by the crystal clear elastic transparency of Futurist Optimism.

F. T. Marinetti, 1930

194. *Summer.* (1925). Oil on tapestry cloth, 91 x 56 1/8 inches. Collection Galleria dell'Obelisco, Rome. Balla executed five painted tapestries for the International Exhibition of Decorative Art, "Art Déco," in Paris in 1925. In each tapestry the composition is inspired by flowers and appears bilaterally symmetrical although the sides are not precisely symmetrical. Warm color tones suggest burnt vegetation in the dry summer heat.

He divided the color of a spout of water and of a ray of sunlight. He fixed on canvas the mathematical, geometric, and luminous Divisionism of the vibrating prism of a great arc lamp. Scientific painter, who painted authentic self-moods and mediumistic fluids of invisible reality, he molded the magic fan of a running automobile which passes quickly before the eyes. He painted the wheel in flight, the vitreous speed of the windows, the shedding of the background field, organizing on canvas these pictorial flashes with masterly unity.

Fortunato Depero:
"In Praise of Giacomo Balla"
(*Gloria a Giacomo Balla*)
in *Dinamo Futurista*, March 1933.

195. Balla, center (wearing one of his Futurist ties), with Jannelli, a giornalist (on the right, wearing a Futurist gillet by Depero), and Depero photographed at the top of the Eiffel Tower in 1925. They had gone to Paris to attend the International Exhibition, "Art Déco," of Decorative Art. Depero, a Futurist painter, was co-author with Balla of the manifesto, "The Futurist Reconstruction of the Universe" (1915).

The decorative art of Balla, that is without doubt the most original achievement of modern Italy, is nothing more than a continuation and application of the ideas, of the experiences, of the temperament, and of the vision of Balla as painter.

Not everyone realizes the upsetting effect which this has had on women's fashions, on interior design, on furniture, on the furnishings of the modern house, on the structure and form of objects, on toys, on lampshades, etc. Above all, Balla can take credit for the new boldness of conception which is beginning to be manifest in the industry of applied arts, and in that large, courageous movement, the most typical examples can be seen in the International Exposition of Decorative Arts in Paris (1925), examples which, from the first to the last, reflect the direct influence which the personality of Italian Futurism has excerised over the European avant-garde.

Guglielmo Gannelli, Luciano Nicastro, in *Sicialia Nuova*, 1925-26.

195

196-99. Four tapestries. (1925). Diluted colors painted on tapestry cloth, each 47 1/4 x 47 1/4 inches. Collection Balla, Rome. In each of the four tapestries, a different species of parrot is depicted; their squawking noises are represented by the irregular zigzag forms around the borders. These noise forms are also to be found coiling around the parrots, and issuing from their beaks. A monkey, rendered in dynamic Futurist lines, swings through the upper left tapestry, while a serpent provokes the parrots' chatter in the tapestry on the lower right. Balla studied these animals from life in the Roman zoo which was within walking distance of his studio.

200. *The Arrows of Life*. (1928). Oil on wood, 35 1/2 x 39 3/8 inches. Collection Balla, Rome. A thicket is the point of departure for this abstract-symbolic painting. Destiny, that measures everything, is represented by a carpenter's rule. The shafts or tree-like forms are the obstacles that hinder us. At left center, the arrows pointing in different directions stand for conflicting ambitions. Evil, in the form of a coiling streamer slithers in and out. The two red heart shapes symbolize love; as the coiling streamer approaches them it takes on their color. The dark greens of the underbrush are snares. The transparent light given off by the carpenter's rule represents happy people, while the suffering are represented by the dark areas in the lower right. Balla himself carved and painted the yellow and green frame with its words and phrases: "The Arrows of Life" (top); "Idealism, Art" (right); "Struggles, Snares, Obstacles" (bottom); "Ambition, Love" (left).

201

201. *Study for the décor of the Löwenstein House, Düsseldorf.* (1912). Ink on paper, 31 1/2 x 47 1/4 inches. Collection Balla, Rome.

202

MOBILE SMONTABILE

Balla's Futurist Universe:
Just as Balla attempted to express Futurist ideas in clothing, he was equally concerned with bringing Futurist vitality to all aspects of modern life. The following ten pages illustrate some of Balla's projects for interiors, for furniture, for clothing, etc., as well as photographs of some of the actual objects. Balla conceived his designs, as composite units so that they could be easily mass-produced and available to the public at large. In 1918 Balla, wrote:

THE FUTURIST UNIVERSE

Any shop in a large modern city with its elegant windows, where objects for use and pleasure are displayed, gives far more aesthetic pleasure than all the highly praised traditional exhibitions. An electric iron, metallic white, smooth, shining, immaculate, delights the eye more than the little nude statuette placed on a shapeless pedestal, stained for the occasion. A typewriter is more architectonic than the building projects which have received awards in academies and competitions. The display window of a perfumer's shop, with its big and little boxes, its large and small bottles whose brightly Futurist colors are multiplied by elegant mirrors; the skilful and attractive design of ladies' shoes; the bizzare ingenuity of little multicolored umbrellas; furriers; leathergoods shops; kitchenware: all these give a greater pleasure to the eye than the grimy little paintings hanging by nails on the gray wall of the traditional painter.
(Reproduced in the catalogue: *Giacomo Balla*, Galleria Civica d'Arte Moderna, Turin, 1963, p. 202).

Rome 1918.

202. Design for a large Futurist cabinet. (c. 1920). Watercolor on paper, 11 1/2 x 8 inches. Collection Balla, Rome. It was to be painted yellow, white and dark blue with a pinkish-violet border. Made of interlocking planes, it could be easily mounted and dismounted.

203

204

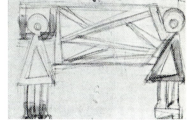

204a

205. A decorative screen (c. 1916-1920). Oil on
wood, painted on both sides in bright colors.
204. Original design for the *Children's Room*.
(1914). Pencil and blue and green watercolor on
paper, 17 1/2 x 22 3/8 inches. Collection Balla,
Rome. Note that the motif for the furniture is
based on various positions of childrens bodies;
the heads and feet are most obvious.
204a. Sketch for a crib in the *Children's Room*.
(1914). Pencil and ink on paper, 8 5/8 x 11 3/8
inches. Collection Balla, Rome.
205. A photograph of the *Children's Room* (1914)
as it was actually constructed. The colors are
blue green and white.

205

206

207

208

206. Design for a Futurist dress creating the effect of projecting cubes. (1925). Watercolor on paper, 7 x 5 inches. Collection Balla, Rome. The background is turquoise, and the cubes are beige and brown outlined in pink.

207. Design for an outfit for the mountains. (c. 1925). Watercolor on paper, 7 x 5 inches. Collection Balla, Rome. The main colors are blue, lavander and white.

208. Design for a Futurist swimming suit. (c. 1925). Watercolor on paper, 7x5 inches. Collection Balla, Rome. The background is ultramarine blue with a motif of red Futurist fish.

209. A black and white silk scarf with automobiles as motif, painted on "fisciu" silk by Luce Balla. The design is Balla's (c. 1930).

210. A blue silk scarf using a motif airplanes, which he had earlier studied as a subject for his paintings.

209

210

...In Italy, Balla was the first to attempt to give the home a sense of well-being, of novelty and of tidiness which did not make one nostalgic for the mediocrity of the other traditional and modern styles which are only cumbersome and useless. He presented his painted panels, his upholstered furniture, his lampshades, his Futurist flowers and vases, his colored and square-sectioned walking sticks, his embroidered fabrics, his painted furniture, which can be dismantled and reassembled so as to adapt through various combinations to transformations of environment. He designed the highly successful decorations for the house of Marinetti, in Piazza Adriana 30, Rome... Today, when ladies choose their clothes they look for the most distinctive forms and the brightest colors. Fabrics are all fantastic interlacements of colored patterns which bear the most obvious imprint of the Futurist experiments. Now it was Balla who, in 1914, amidst the astonishment and the jeers of the Italians, launched the very first brightly-colored fabrics which even to this day are considered the "non plus ultra" of novelty and elegance. It was Balla who eliminated from neckties those stupid solid colors that smelled of old age, resignation, fear, weakness and tobacco. Balla is a physiognomist; he wants to know man not only by his face and gesture, but, above all, by the way he dresses, by the colors and the furnishings for his dwelling. He places great importance on these factors for the destiny and value of individuals... A home decorated by Balla forces one to be intuitive, agile and alert; it leads one to discussions, good humour and, if you like, even to a happy married life.

Guglielmo Jannelli, Luciano Nicastro: "L'Arte Decorativa di Balla." From *Sicilia Nuova*, c. 1925-26.

211. Futurist shoes designed by Balla about 1914. Black on white paper, 4 3/4 x 9 1/2 inches.
212. "Modifiers" in colored felt to be applied to one's clothes, according to one's mood. The modifier on the right includes the "line of force" (triangular) and the curved "line of velocity." On the left is an interpenetrating flower motif.

211

212

213

213. A hammered aluminum belt buckle on wood, and a bracelet made of bamboo with overlaid beaten aluminum designs (c. 1920-25).
214. Balla's own Futurist vest, designed by him and embroidered by his daughter Luce (c. 1920). The colors are two tones of violet, blue, dark blue, and wine red.

214

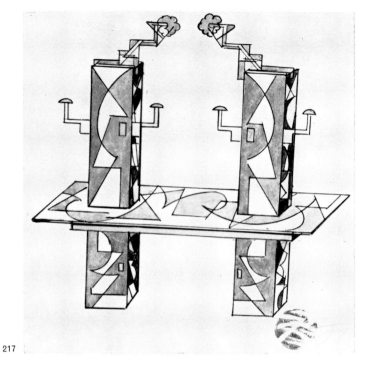

217

215

216

218

219

220

215. A Futurist Interior. (c. 1918). Watercolor on paper, 11 3/4 x 9 inches. An arrow points to a lamp incorporated into the decoration of the walls and ceiling. In the Futurist desk-bench combination, there is an indirect lamp. Such subtle illumination was quite modern compared to the traditional and centralized lamp fixture with its direct lighting.

216. *Villa Borghese - Summer Landscape.* (1926). Oil on wood, 41 1/4 x 41 1/4 inches. Collection Balla, Rome. Using earlier visual experiences of Villa Borghese, Balla made several large designs for embroideries. (He also designed many using the sea and ships as motifs).

217. Design for a hat rack (c. 1918). Watercolor on paper, 11 1/2 x 17 3/4 inches. The colors are white, yellow, light and dark blue. The upper and lower portions opened for storage space.

218. *La Settimana Romana.* (1920). Tempera on paper, 15 3/4 x 11 3/4 inches. The colors are predominantly reds and yellows. It was to be the cover of a magazine called "La Settimana Romana," the letters of which are the basis for Balla's design.

219. A mobile in shades of blue (c. 1925-30) based on Balla's study of flowers. 14 1/2 inches in diameter.

220. A screen painted for the Principessa Caetani (c. 1925-30, present whereabouts unknown). The Principessa Caetani published an international literary magazine called *Botteghe Oscure.*

221

223

222

224

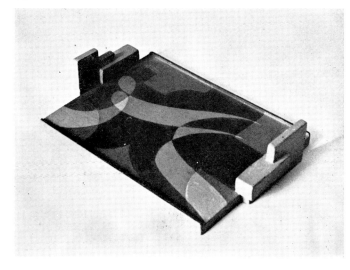

221. Upholstered wooden stool painted in green and yellow for Balla's dining room in Via Paisiello (c. 1918).

222. Small wooden table painted in green and yellow, part of the same dining room (c. 1918). 20 3/4 x 14 3/8 inches.

223. Giacomo Balla photographed by the author in his studio in 1952. The sideboard and the chair had formed part of the dining-room furniture in his studio-apartment in Via Paisiello about 1918. The original dining-room décor had been painted by Balla in the colors of the landscape; the sideboard was painted in yellow and green, while the walls had been of an intense blue over which an orange "line of velocity" had been superimposed.

224. Painted wooden tray for Balla's dining room (c. 1918). 9 1/4 x 12 3/8 inches. The colors are green and yellow.

225. One side of an obelisk-shaped lampshade for the dining room in Via Paisiello. Colored ink on paper, 25 1/2 inches high. It is decorated with the same "line of velocity" motif which had been painted by Balla on the walls. On the lower foreground of the lampshade are two superimposed images of the dining-room chair motif. (See fig. 227).

226. *Strange Man's Chair*. (c. 1930). Oil on canvas, 21 1/4 x 29 3/8 inches. Collection Bajocchi, Rome. Balla portrayed one of his dining-room chairs (fig. 227) realistically in the foreground of a semi-abstract ambient. In the background, Balla has represented himself as a stick figure. In the distance are the buildings of Monte Mario as he saw them from his window. This is a self-portrait of Balla in his private world.

227. One of Balla's dining-rooms chairs (c. 1918). One of a series of twelve chairs for the dingin room on Via Paisiello. Painted wood, 40 1/2 x 17 3/4 x 14 1-2 inches.

225

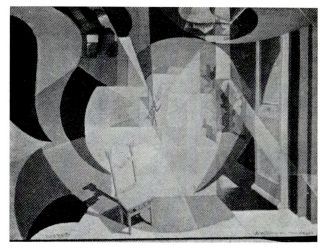
226

227

228

230   229

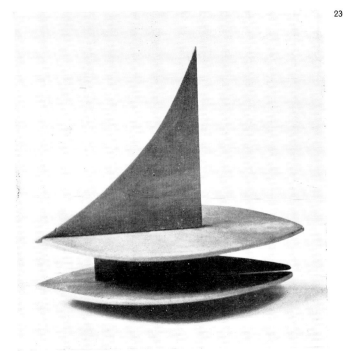

228. Balla's hammered metal tray for salt and pepper, oil and vinegar.

229. Balla's own Futurist walking sticks and umbrella stand which he made himself.

230. A boat-shaped jewel stand designed by Balla for a cousin who loved the sea. The entire wooden object is covered with his painted seascape impressions which are barely visible in the photograph.

231. Painted wood egg-holders and an egg-cup. Note the Futurist cut-out silhouette of chickens.

232. A Futurist letter-holder. The abstract shapes recall the dynamic forms and "lines of force" in such paintings as *Pessimism and Optimism*.

233. Balla made and painted a number of table-top easels to hold small paintings.

234. Futurist coat-hangars made and painted by Balla.

231

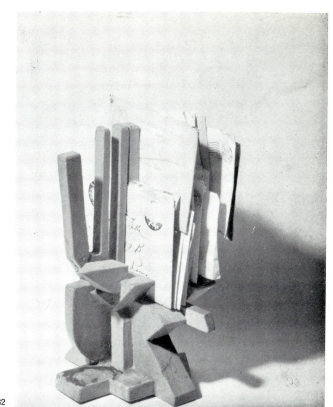

232

233

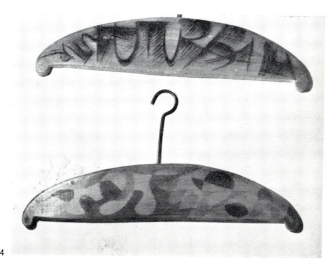

234

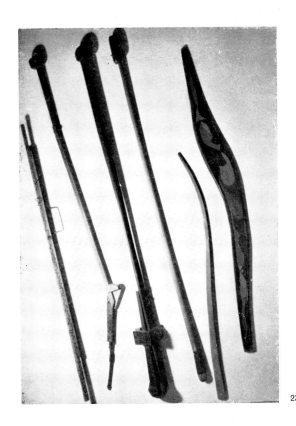

235

236

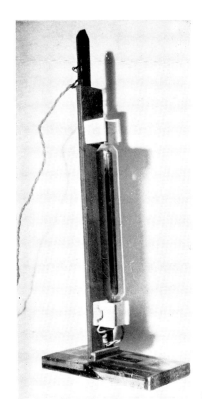

237

238

235. Mall sticks, charcoal holders and other instruments made by Balla.

236. A six-foot extension brush-holder for painting very large canvases and ceilings.

237. Electric work light with elongated bulb. Balla designed this as a portable lamp he could put by his feet when painting.

238. Balla's personal compass, always on his working table.

239-240-241. Brushes carved by Balla. The horsehair and pig bristles were supplied by people with whom Balla had made friends while on painting excursions in the Roman countryside.

242. Balla liked to construct his own tools, which he then used in making sculpture, furniture, picture frames and stretchers. Often, used packing cases provided the wood for his carpentry.

243. Balla's handmade hammer and plane.

244. A paint box built by Balla.

239

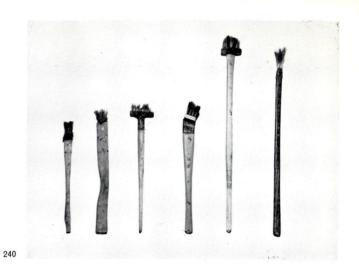

240

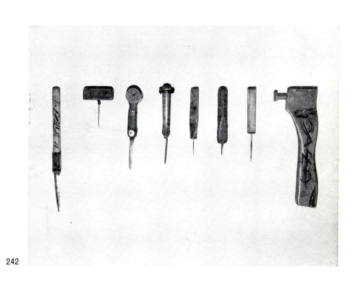

241

242

243

244

BALLA wrote in 1927:

HOW TO FEEL LIKE A FUTURIST (extract)

In order to feel like a Futurist, one has to be imbued with an intuitive sensitivity and slip furtively between those imperceptible moments of evolution in order to discover new ways leading to the Futurist art in which no concept, no line, no form, no color, no shape, no phrase, no musical note shall ever recall the slightest, and I mean the very slightest, element of past art. The Futurist of today will also destroy all atavism by being in contact with aviation, sports, motoring, radio-telegraphy, mechanics, new sciences, precious material still in an embryonic stage, important factor in the development of art of the future. The wars to come, terribly destructive to men and things, shall disinfect the world of all traditional conservatism.

Some ironic soul will observe that, after all these statements, everything will remain more or less like before! ... True ... and yet not true ... because if a hundredth part is the beginning of a million, and the millimeter of a kilometer, even the most modest Futurist attempts may be the beginning of the new art of the future. And so, with indestructible superhope, I say: "See you again in a few centuries."

From: Vetrina Futurista, Ediz. Sindacati Artistici, Turin (1927). Reprinted in the Turin Catalogue, 1963, pp. 204-205.

245. In 1929, Balla was photographed in his Futurist suit of black, turquoise and yellow. The colossal green hand behind him is a detail of a huge painting by Balla portraying his own hands. (Collection Balla, Rome).

246. In 1947, Balla, working in his studio, is photographed by Gjon Mili who had brought him one of his stroboscopic photographs of dancers.

247. Overleaf: Giacomo Balla was photographed by the author in his studio in 1952 as he made free-line drawings from memory. To the right of the photograph is Balla's Futurist cabinet and the upper portion of his dining-room chair.

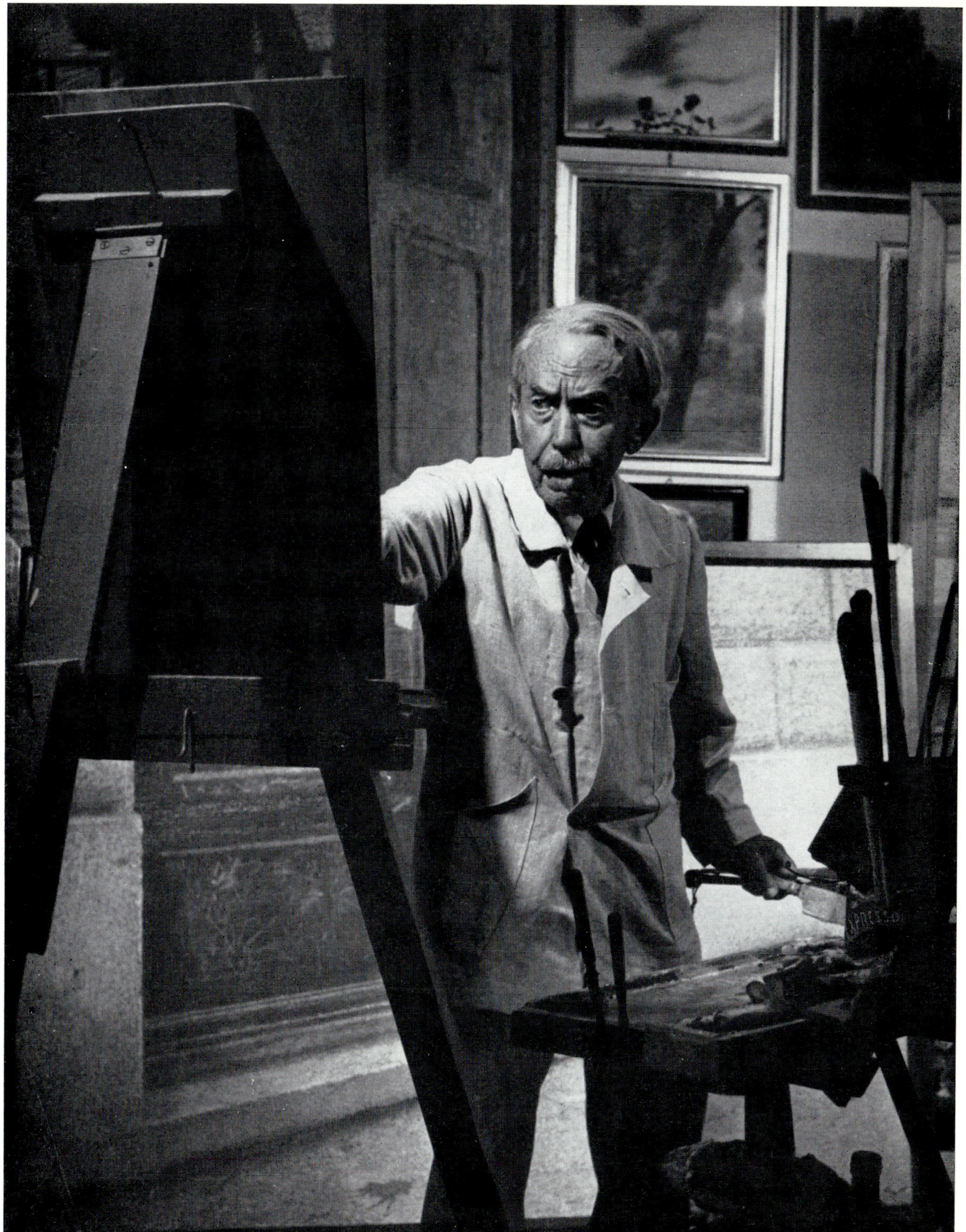

A preface written by F.T. Marinetti for the catalogue of Balla's one-man exhibition in 1930 at the Galleria del Dipinto, Rome. The show was also inaugurated by Marinetti on June 22nd.

I consider the painter Giacomo Balla a typically Turinese genius. In fact, with the love of geometric order and the tenacious industry which are characteristic of the Piedmont capitol, Balla organized and regimented his tumultuous creative energy. He was born in 1871 in Turin, of Turinese parents, on one of those great tree-lined boulevards which, opening in wide vistas onto the infinite, frame distant plains, hills and mountains with their dazzling glaciers, as if preparing for an artillery shot. These things taught him the plastic and spiritual value of space and kindled in his young muscles the urge to travel on land, on sea, and in the sky, following the most unbridled fantasies.

At the age of twenty-five, having moved to Rome, he is not affected by the languid atmosphere and the nostalgia for glorious ashes. His mother, an intelligent and iron-willed working-class woman, seated near his easel, makes sure that the fragrance of the gardens does not slacken his agile brush; with Piedmont tenacity, her son must put on canvas all the magic of Roman light.

He bears in his heart the square plazas of Turin, all filled with summer sun or December snow, and they keep him firmly attached to constructive reality. Monuments to glorious Kings, cloaked in mist, still gallop through his memory. His pulse still beats to the military formation of the electric street-lamps marching between high buildings, against a sky already defeated in its disorder. That is how he began his hard life as a great innovating painter, committed to pressing and moulding the incandescent Beauty of the Modern Era like a steel-press.

Frugal, sober, shy of glory, he is like an ambitious lonely peak with its pebbles made precious by the sun and the wind, with its clouds and its familiar stars. He had the garrulous thoughtlessness of a young man who jokes with flowers and the rosy little feet of children. Late at night, lying on his back in the Roman countryside, facing the zenith, he would speak of the costellations and try to steal their formulas and their untranslatable splendor. From the beginning, Balla, a solar spirit, worked unceasingly on the complicated problem of light and, neglecting sentimental values, devised a solidified impressionism of moulded shadows and rays of light. No painter ever attained the force of observation of Balla's eyes.

Twenty years ago, during one of those metallicaly sparkling and yet still balmy September afternoons in Villa Borghese, I had the good fortune to approach him unseen and observe him at length. Standing erect, motionless, wearing an asymmetrical turquoise blue jacket, his arms crossed over a necktie decorated with glass bells and scarlet painted wood, he stared with half-closed eyes at a high fountain iridescent with changing jewels . . .

And off we ran, in the midst of the slating arrows of a barbaric sunset which was fleeing, struggling against the white explosions of electric lights. We looked at them with joy, risking being hit by the automobiles, since Balla loves getting very close to wheels and fenders to taste the danger and train himself to be agile.

In this exhibition I find all the Balla of yester-year in a very original painting entitled: "My Moment." Short of stature, a rapid step which injects itself into the pulp of the crowd. His right hand points the paintbrush while his flashing steel-gray eyes follow the windswept gray smoke of his diabolical hair which has certainly escaped from the live palette projecting from three fingers of his left had. A lightning-quick brush stroke is made on the bound while his mouth prolongs the burlesque contorsion of a word howled right and left at possible jeering critics, simultaneously, at home and in the street, his walking stick paints and stabs the air, projecting foreward a red cone of willpower. On his head, like a magician's hat, he wears another cone of red light as he walks regally amidst the immense multi-colored blocks of the new dream cities whose buildings run along tracks of interpenetrating light-rays. This is the same smiling, agile and enthusiastic Balla who twenty years ago fought with first and cane against the traditionalists on the stage of the Costanzi Theater. He is always ready to share ideas, soup and colors with the young artists, as he was in those days on the high gallery of his first studio on Via Porpora, the quarter-deck of a long transatlantic house which truly seemed to set sail under his Futurist commands.

The painter Giacomo Balla surpasses and shatters every definition. How can one describe his repainting the earth? Compare him to someone, something? Impossible... the traditional poets seek in vain to find a definition. Liquidation of the entire metaphoric style. Balla, greatest painter of today, is like a storm cloud bristling with electricity or even better a cyclone which rampages the ruins. He is a painter gifted with an extraordinary manual dexterity. His initial passion for realistic precision drove him to an almost religious study of objects down to their very pores and in their least perceptible aspect. He intensified this capillary observation to the point of delirium. The most delicate chiaroscuro and the subtle transparencies of his early works are even now a world to explore. It is still to be wondered how Balla obtained the marvellous effect of desolation or of tragic misery in his celebrated painting 'Bankrupt' with the minutest details of the closed-down shop's door, all marked with chalk by passers-by. We find just as inexplicable the realism of his portraits of political figures in the Capitol (Rome). But then, when he reaches thirty-eight years old, Balla suffers a violent artistic crisis. The goal he has attained nauseates him. His painting, the 'Worker's Day' reveals, in its spontaneous Divisionism, a deep feeling for the people and, at the same time, an acute desire to escape. Then the Futurist Movement in painting explodes in Rome's theaters, academies and schools, and Balla audaciously takes the lead along with his closest pupil Umberto Boccioni. A stroke of genius is needed to solve the plastic problem of mechanized speed and the electric light. Immediately, he exhibits, before the astonished eyes of his anguished admirers, the polychromed rays of his 'Street Lamp'. The controversies, the derision and the enthusiasm intermingle over 'The Dog on a Leash' which assaulted the critics with its owner's multiple feet, the moving fringe of its little paws, and the elastic transparency of the vibrating leash. Meanwhile Italian cities are thrown into turmoil by the Interventionist movement against Germany and Austria.

Exciting atmosphere of insurrection around the consulate grounds crowded with Carabinieri. Students rioting on the staircase. Neutralists beaten up. Mothers and sisters on balconies overlooking the crowd unwinding in the streets like a gigantic snake swelling with adolescent warriors. Balla is the youngest of the youngsters. He is everywhere in all the Roman streets. All the Futurists camp down in his study. Forgotten are the swallows' flights in pale skies around moaning, pacifist bell towers. He is the scarlet of the revolt. He relaxes by painting the dynamic volumes of patriotic passion. His genius creates the impressionism of a flood of people, stylizing its black waves mingled with threatening yellow streaks, under the solid tricolored cloud symbolizing the song of Italian students. In this phase of Balla's oeuvre which we call Interventionist, he evolves as the creator of 'Mood paintings', the dynamic architect of spiritual environments, the painter capable of putting the mysterious forces of the universe on canvas with synoptic colors.

After the war, predictably and yet miraculously, his masterpiece finally appears: 'Optimism and Pessimism'. Any Italian, who has not yet fathomed the achievements and the infinite possibilities of Futurist painting, can profit by studying the funereal pointed tentacles of traditional Pessimism which will certainly be overcome by the crystal clear elastic transparency of Futurist Optimism.

F. T. Marinetti speaking in a Futurist evening with Folgore and Cangiullo.

GIACOMO BALLA - TURINESE

Temperament: Intuitive daring
Art - Ist Period: personal objective realism — rebel to all academic schools — Analysis of our life — solutions research divisionistic (lights, environments — psyche objects people) — Struggles efforts pleasures — achievements, successful career, recognized by public, artist, critic.
2nd Period — FUTURISM — *evolution: complete disavowal of own work and career. Public, artists, critics stunned — incomprehension — Accusations — insanity — mistrust — derision — pity — Received with smiling indifference — First plastic studies of movement (speeding automobiles, people in motion) public curiosity — laughing insults, mockery, disbelief-violent arguments (poor and great Italians, you were all bursting with a huge indigestion. Pro Germanists!!!).*
Continual research. Definitely renouncing of analysis of reality — Creation of a new Futuri ststyle: synthetic abstract forms, subjective, dynamic.
More searching — struggles.
FUTURISM FOREWARD MARCH...

(Giacomo Balla 1915)

BALLA: The role of traditional and Futurist colors. Dated 1914-1915.

Traditional yellow: depressing, drives one to misery, to begging

Futurist *Yellow* — Joyous: *invites wealth, celebrating, pleasure.*

Traditional green — bilious: *breeds envy, anger, suspicion*

Futurist *Green* — pleasant: *exciting, awakening, fertile, refreshes and makes youthful.*

Traditional blue — monotonous: *affected, indecisive, boring, lazy, inactive.*

Futurist *Blue* — Spiritual: *nourishes the inspiration, awakens desire to travel by sea, in the sky, and on land.*

Traditional red — discouraging: *saps all physical and moral energy.*

Futirist *Red* — Violent: *Stimulates muscles, blood, nerves and brain.*

Traditional violet — mortuary: *puts the mind and heart to sleep, consumes life.*

Futurist *Violet* — Agile-rendering *makes ideas more transparent, caresses love and art.*

Traditional white — dirty: *leads to all that is filthy, infective, ugly, obscurantism.*

Futurist *White* — Clairvoyant: *beautifies, cleanses, clarifies, heals everything and everyone.*

Traditional black — Tottering: *pertaining to the catafalque, smudgy, slow, spreads sadness everywhere.*

Going along Via Paisiello last year I saw that Giacomo Balla's famous house had been torn open by the pick-axe of the demolishers. The spreading out of modern constructions had still left a part standing, but the execution was imminent.

I remember that there still remained part of the long rear balcony, that strange balcony that had been the object of many dynamic observations of the painter who, from the half-closed door of the studio, would peer out at the children running on the noisy slate tiles of the balcony. Multiplication of railing supports, feet, legs, airy swishing of skirts. The surviving wall, with the typical flavor of bared intimacy, surprised me with a huge 'Balla!' written on a slant and leading off into who knows what whirling depths. That was part of the room where Giacomo Balla used to line up the family brooms in perfect order, almost as if they were at ease, after having been used in the dynamism of the landscape. The relentless gap in the walls carried me back to the period when the light inner walls had been the back-drop and the theater of Futurism in Rome. Gatherings, stimulation of brains and wit, in groups of twenty, of thirty, we would all go to Balla's, to see what Balla was up to, to listen to Marinetti at Balla's, to study Balla's discoveries. Balla himself, penetrating, amusing, a-logical and facetious, with a stylized smile between his waxed mustache and chin-whiskers would come in a flash from the endless perspective of communicating rooms: black varnished shoes and light laces, small-checkered trousers, multicolored vest and shirt, dark jacket with purple lapels, a square-cut walking stick and a perfume which Mrs. Balla had devised for afternoons and Sunday occasions. At his sudden appearance the mustache and beard emited a 'neh!' so charmingly nasal and Piedmontese that it has become proverbial among all those who would go there. 'Benone! perdio santino!' (Fine by golly!) and the discussions would begin. Futurist Evenings would take form, artistic dissidences were fomented, and patriotic demonstrations were organized. Paintings cluttered up every available space on the floor, hanging on the wall one above the other, leaning on shiny plastic constructions, hanging from the ceiling, hooked onto wire like laundry hung out to dry, or better, like flags which made the air, and our heads, giddy.

(Extract from an article on G.B. written by Virgilio Marchi, and published in 'La Stirpe', March 1928, Rome)

F.T. MARINETTI
BRUNO CORRA
E. SETTIMELLI
G. BALLA
REMO CHITI

THE FUTURIST CINEMA

Futurist Manifesto published in the 9th issue of the newspaper L'Italia Futurista

11th September, 1916

The book, that traditional medium for preserving and communicating ideas, has long been — like cathedrals, towers, battlemented walls, museums and pacifist ideals — destined to disappear. The book, static companion of the sedentary, nostalgic and neutralist man, can neither amuse nor excite the new futurist generations roused by revolutionary, bellicose dynamism. The outbreak of war is sharpening European sensitivity. Our great hygienic war, besides fulfilling *all* our national aspirations, will increase the renovating power of the Italian race. The futurist cinema we are working on is a joyful deformation of the universe, an illogical and flashing synthesis of world life. It will become the best school for our youth: a school of joy, speed, strength, fearlessness and heroism. The futurist cinema will sharpen our sensitivity, develop our creative imagination and it will give our intelligence a prodigious sense of simultaneity and omnipresence.

The Futurist cinema will thus help in the general renewal, substituting magazines (always pedantic), plays (always predictable) and killing books (always tedious and oppressive).

The need for propaganda will force us to publish a book now and then, but we prefer to express ourselves through the cinema, through free-ranging words on big canvases and through the language of movement and light.

Our Manifesto 'The Synthetic Futurist Theatre', the successful tours of Gualtiero Tumati's, Ettore Berti's, Annibale Ninchi's and Luigi Zoncada's theatre companies, and the two volumes on the Synthetic Futurist Theatre containing 80 theatrical syntheses, have originated the revolution of the theatre in Italy. Previously, another futurist manifesto had rehabilitated, glorified and perfected the Variety Theatre. It is logical, therefore, that we should now aim our life-giving efforts at another realm of the theatre: the cinema.

At first sight the cinema — only recently invented — may seem a born futurist, that is: without a past, and free from tradition. But in fact, emerging as a *theatre without words*, the cinema has inherited all the most traditional garbage of the literary theatre. We can, therefore, apply to the cinema all we have said about and done for the theatre. Our undertaking is legitimate and necessary, for the cinema *has been so far, and looks like it will continue to be, deeply traditional*, while we see in it the possibility of an eminently futurist art, and consider it to be the most suitable means of expression for the plurisensitivity of a futurist artist.

Except for a few interesting shorts on travelling, hunting, war, etc., we have been dished out nothing but unbearably traditional dramas, tragedies and melodramas. The script itself — which, because of its concise form, may appear to be progressive — in most cases is nothing more than a pitiful and trite *analysis*. Therefore, the immense artistic potential of the cinema is still conpletely untapped.

The cinema is an art form in its own right. It must never imitate the stage. The cinema — being essentially visual — must above all evolve the way painting has done and move away from reality, from photography, from the pretty and from the solemn. It must become anti-pretty, deforming, impressionistic, synthetic, dynamic, 'parolibero'. *It is necessary to free the cinema as a means of expression* in order to turn it into the ideal instrument of *a new art form*, an art form that will be more flexible and on a larger scale than all the others. We are convinced that only through the cinema will it be possible to achieve the *polyexpressiveness* sought by all modern artistic efforts. Today, in fact, the *futurist cinema* creates the *polyexpressive symphony* which we announced in our manifesto a year ago: *é Weights, measures and prices of the artistic genius*. The futurist film will be made up of the most varied expressive elements: from the slice of life to the splash of color, from single lines to free-ranging words, from chromatic and plastic music to the music of objects.

In short, it will be painting, architecture, sculpture, free-ranging words, music of colors, lines and shapes, medley of objects and reality turned into chaos. We shall offer new inspiration to the painters who tend to strain the limits of their canvases. We shall put into motion the free-ranging words that burst the limits of literature and march on towards painting, music and the art of noise-making, spanning a wonderful bridge between the word and the real object.

Our films will be:

1. *Filmed analogies*, using reality as one of the two elements of analogy. For example: in wanting to show the distress of our hero, we will not describe it through its various stages, but present its equivalent impression by showing an indented and cavernous mountain.

Mountains, seas, woods, cities, crowds, armies, squads, airplanes these will frequently be our most expressive words: *The universe will be our vocabulary*.

For example, in wanting to express a feeling of strange mirth, we shall show a group of chairs whirling merrily round an enormous cloak-stand till they decide to hang on it. In wanting to express a feeling of wrath, we shall bombard the wrathful one with a multitude of yellow bullets. In wanting to express the distress of a Hero about to lose his faith in the funereal scepticism of the neutralists, we shall show the inspired Hero as he speaks to a crowd, then we suddenly show Giovanni Giolitti as he treacherously pushes a forkful of succulent macaroni into the Hero's mouth, thus drowning his lofty words in tomato sauce.

We shall enrich dialogues by showing quickly and simultaneously all the images that cross the character's mind. For example, a man says to his girl: 'You are as beautiful as a gazelle'. We shall show a gazelle. A character says: 'I watch your fresh and luminous smile as a traveller at the end of a tiring journey watches the sea from the top of a mountain'. We shall show traveler, sea and mountain.

Thus it will be perfectly easy to understand our characters, it will be as though they *were actually speaking*.

2. *Filmed poems and speeches*. We shall show on the screen all the images that make them up. For example: 'Love song' by Giosuè Carducci.
'Perched high on German rocks
like hawks planning the kill'
We shall show rocks and hawks lying in wait.
'In churches that stretch marble arms
up to the sky, they pray to God'.
'In convents standing gloomily, in hamlets
and towns, amidst chiming bells,
like so many owls on thinned-out trees
singing of boredom and of strange mirth'.
We shall show churches as they gradually turn into imploring women, a delighted God in the skies, convents, owls, etc.
For example: 'Summer Dream' by Giosue Carducci.
'In the heat of battles, ringing forever through

your poems, Homer, I was overcome:
sleep won me over and my head rested
on the Scamandrous shores, but my
heart flew out to the Tyrrhenian sea'.
We shall show Carducci wondering among the turmoil of the Achaei, skilfully avoiding the galloping horses, paying his respects to Homer, going into the Red Scamandrous inn to have a drink with Ajax and, at the third glass of wine, his heart — the beating of which must be seen — bursting out of his coat and flying away towards Rapallo bay like a red balloon. This way we film the most secret movement of genius. Thus we shall ridicule the works of traditional poets, turning even the most nostalgically monotonous and tear-jerking poems into exciting, violent and exhilarating shows for the benefit of the spectators.

3. *Filmed simultaneity and interpenetration* of time and places. We shall present 2 or 3 different visions in the same instant-shot.

4. *Filmed musical experiments* (dissonances, chords, symphonies of gestures, facts, colors, lines, etc.).

5. *Filmed scripted states of mind*.

6. *Filmed daily exercises to get rid of logic*.

7. *Filmed object dramas*. (Animated, humanized, made-up, dressed, civilized, dancing objects — objects invested with passions, removed from their usual place and forced into an abnormal condition that — by contrast — will show up their astonishing construction and non-human existence).

8. *Filmed showcases of ideas*, *events*, *types*, *objects*, *etc*.

9. *Filmed congresses*, *flirts*, *brawls*, *marriages of grimaces*, *miming*, *etc*.
For example: a huge nose silencing a thousand fingers at a Congress by ringing an ear, while two policeman's moustaches arrest a tooth.

10. *Filmed unreal re-constructions of the human body*.

11. *Filmed dramas of disproportions*. (A thirsty man taking out a straw that grows like an umbilical cord, plunges into a lake and sucks it dry).

12. *Filmed potential dramas and strategic plans for feelings*.

13. *Filmed linear*, *plastic*, *chromatic equivalences*, *etc*., with men, women, events, thoughts, music, weights, smells, noises. (We shall show, with white lines on black, the interior and physical rhythm of a husband finding his wife with her lover and chasing the lover — rhythm of his soul and of his legs).

14. *Filmed free-ranging words in motion* (synoptic tables of lyrical values — dramas of humanized and animalized letters — orthographic dramas — typographic dramas — geometrical dramas - nu-

meric sensitivity, etc.).

Painting + sculpture + plastic dynamism + free-ranging words + noise tuning + architecture + synthetic theatre = futurist cinema. *We break up and recompose the Universe according to our wonderful whims* in order to centuplicate the Italian creative genius and its absolute supremacy over the world.

Note: Balla partecipated in the first Futurist film (1916) called « Vita Futurista» as both author and actor.

SELECTED BIBLIOGRAPHY

Balla:

Calvesi, Maurizio. 'Penetrazione e Magia nella Pittura di Balla', *L'Arte è Moderna*, n. 40, vol. V (1967).

Crispolti, Enrico and Gambillo Drudi, Maria. *Giacomo Balla*, Catalogue, Galleria Civica d'Arte Moderna, Turin, April 4, 1963.

Depero, Fortunato. 'Gloria a Giacomo Balla', *Dinamo Futurista*, (March, 1933).

Fagiolo, Maurizio. *Balla: le 'compenetrazioni iridescenti'*, Rome, 1968.

Fagiolo, Maurizio. *Balla pre-futurista*, Rome, 1968.

Fagiolo, Maurizio. *Omaggio a Balla*, Rome, 1967.

Fagiolo, Marizio. *Balla: ricostruzione futurista dell'universo*, Rome, 1968.

Jannelli, Guglielmo and Nicastro, Luciano. 'L'Arte Decorativa di Balla', *Sicilia Nuova*, (1925-26).

Marchi, Virgilio. 'Giacomo Balla', *La Stirpe*, Rome (March, 1928).

Marinetti, F.T. Preface to the catalogue of Balla's one-man exhibition at the Galleria del Dipinto, Rome, 1930.

Futurism:

Calvesi, Maurizio. 'Antologia Critica, Bibliografia e Indici del Volume Quinto', *L'Arte Moderna*, n. 45, vol. V (1967).

Calvesi, Maurizio. 'Il Futurismo Romano', *L'Arte Moderna*, n. 41, vol. V (1967).

Calvesi, Maurizio. 'Il Manifesto del Futurismo e i Pittori Futuristi', *L'Arte Moderna*, n. 37, vol. V (1967).

Calvese, Maurizio. *L'Arte Moderna*, n. 40, vol. V. (1968).

Drudi Gambillo, M. and Fiori, T. Archivi del Futurismo, voll. 2, Rome,

Taylor, Joshua C. *Futurism*. The Museum of Modern Art, New York, 1961.

General:

Bragaglia, Giulio Anton. *Foto Dinamismo Futurista*, Rome, 1912.

Dorazio, Piero. *La Fantasia dell'Arte nella Vita Moderna*, Rome, 1955.

Minnaert, M. *Light and Colour*, New York, 1954.

Moholy-Nagy, L. *Vision in Motion*, Chicago, 1947.

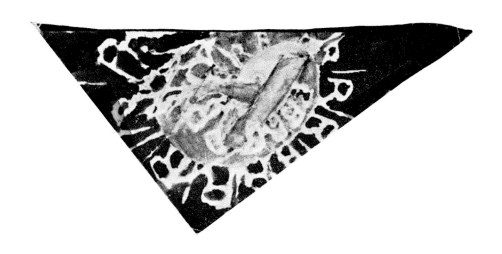